AROUND **chicago** WITH *KIDS*

by Nancy Maes

Fodor's Travel Publications
New York • Toronto • London • Sydney • Auckland

www.fodors.com

CREDITS
Writer: Nancy Maes

Series Editors: Karen Cure, Caroline Haberfeld
Editor: Andrea Lehman
Editorial Production: Linda Schmidt
Production/Manufacturing: Robert Shields

Design: Fabrizio La Rocca, *creative director*;
Tigist Getachew, *art director*
Illustration and Series Design: Rico Lins, Keren Ora
Admoni/Rico Lins Studio

ABOUT THE WRITER
Nancy Maes, author of the *Chicago Tribune*'s "Family Fare"
column, is also the mother of two sons.

First Edition
ISBN 0-679-00488-2
ISSN 1526-1379

Important Tip
Although all prices, opening times, and other details in this
book are based on information supplied to us at press time,
changes occur all the time in the travel world, and Fodor's
cannot accept responsibility for facts that become outdated
or for inadvertent errors or omissions. So always confirm
information when it matters, especially if you're making a
detour to visit a specific place.

Special Sales
Fodor's Travel Publications are available at special discounts
for bulk purchases for sales promotions or premiums. Special
editions, including personalized covers, excerpts of existing
guides, and corporate imprints, can be created in large
quantities for special needs. For more information, contact
your local bookseller or Special Markets, Fodor's Travel
Publications, 201 East 50th Street, New York, NY 10022.
Inquiries from Canada should be directed to your local
Canadian bookseller or sent to Random House of Canada,
Ltd., Marketing Dept., 2775 Matheson Boulevard East,
Mississauga, Ontario L4W 4P7. Inquiries from the United
Kingdom should be sent to Fodor's Travel Publications, 20
Vauxhall Bridge Road, London, England SW1V 2SA.

PRINTED IN THE UNITED STATES OF AMERICA
10 9 8 7 6 5 4 3 2 1

CONTENTS

WELCOME TO GREAT DAYS!

Between pick-ups, drop-offs, and after-school activities, organizing a family's schedule is one full-time job. Planning for some fun time together shouldn't be another. That's where this book helps out. In creating it, our parent-experts have done all the legwork, so you don't have to. Open to any page and you'll find a great day together already planned out. You can read about the main event, check our age-appropriateness ratings to make sure it's right for your family, pick up some smart tips, and find out where to grab a bite nearby.

HOW TO SAVE MONEY
Taking a whole family on an outing can be pricey, but there are ways to save.

1. Always ask about discounts at ticket booths. We list admission prices only for adults and kids, but an affiliation (and your ID) may get you a break. If you want to support a specific institution, consider buying a family membership up front. Usually these pay for themselves after a couple of visits, and sometimes they come with other good perks—gift-shop and parking discounts, and so on.

2. Keep an eye peeled for coupons. They'll save you $2 or $3 a head and you can find them everywhere from the supermarket to your pediatrician's office. Combination tickets, sometimes offered by groups of attractions, cost less than if you pay each admission individually.

3. Try to go on free days. Some attractions let you in at no charge one day a month or one day a week after a certain time.

GOOD TIMING

Most attractions with kid appeal are busy when school is out. Field-trip destinations are sometimes swamped on school days, but these groups tend to leave by early afternoon, so weekdays after 2 during the school year can be an excellent time to visit museums, zoos, and aquariums. Outdoors, consider going after a rain—there's nothing like a downpour to clear away crowds. If you go on a holiday, call ahead—we list only the usual operating hours.

SAFETY CATCH

Take a few sensible precautions. Show your kids how to recognize staff or security people when you arrive. And designate a meeting time and place—some visible landmark—in case you become separated. It goes without saying that you should keep a close eye on your children at all times, especially if they are small.

FINAL THOUGHTS

We'd love to hear yours: What did you and your kids think about the places we recommend? Have you found other places we should include? Send us your ideas via e-mail (c/o editors@fodors.com, specifying the name of this book on the subject line) or snail mail (c/o Around Chicago with Kids, Fodor's Travel Publications, 201 East 50th Street, New York, NY 10022). In the meantime, have a great day around Chicago with your kids!

THE EDITORS

ADLER PLANETARIUM AND
ASTRONOMY MUSEUM

68

Change in the universe is slow, but change in the way we view it and understand it doesn't have to be. This six-decades-old planetarium has kept up with the times, offering star gazers both low-tech and high-tech means of exploring the heavens.

Start in the History of Astronomy Galleries to see items used over the centuries to explore the universe. Kids interested in astronomy the way it used to be can step into the restored Atwood Sphere. Predating the 1930 planetarium, the big steel sphere was once part of the Chicago Academy of Sciences. Small holes allow light in, simulating Chicago's night sky in 1913, complete with the movements of planets. If your children want a splendid view of Chicago and its sky today, check out the new semicircular, glass-enclosed addition, which overlooks Lake Michigan; a ground-level telescope yields a close-up look at celestial objects. The Gateway to the Universe will transport them in a different way. Here they can take a space walk, discovering the roles of light, gravity, motion, and energy.

KID-FRIENDLY EATS An expanse of windows overlooks Lake Michigan and the sky above at **Galileo's,** the planetarium's restaurant. It serves reasonably priced pizzas, pastas, and salads with an upscale touch and, for fussy eaters, hot dogs and peanut butter sandwiches.

KEEP IN MIND Very young children may be more frightened than enthralled by the sky shows, and StarRider, in particular, may overwhelm youngsters. The more conventional Zeiss Sky Theater, however, offers a low-key show that takes into account the interests and sensibilities of 3- to 5-year-olds. Called "The Littlest Dinosaur," it plays at 10:30 from Memorial Day weekend through Labor Day weekend and at 11:30 during the other months.

1300 S. Lake Shore Dr.

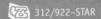 312/922-STAR

$5 adults, $4 children 4–17; T free;
Zeiss Sky Theater $5; StarRider $5

June–Labor Day, Th–F 9–9, Sa–W 9–6; early
Sept--May, M–Th 9–5, F 9–9, Sa–Su 9–6

3 and up

At other exhibits your children put on 3-D glasses and experience the Milky Way as though they were really there (which, of course, they are) and step into a solar observatory. Sophisticated sky shows are in store in the Zeiss Sky Theater, here since the planetarium opened. But the museum's pièce de résistance is the domed StarRider Theater, the first of its kind. Using the same technology used to train pilots and astronauts in flight simulators, it enables kids, and adults, to really imagine themselves as colonists on Mars. First, audience members make decisions, such as where to set up a colony and what kind of shelter to build. Next, would-be colonists recline in their chairs and "depart" on a thrilling customized adventure, watching as 60 3-D images a second are projected onto the ceiling.

And when all the wizardry is over, you may want to close your day in appreciative silence by gazing up at the night sky.

HEY, KIDS! Do you know what "spaghettifying" means? No, it's not some horrifying pasta experiment. It's a phenomenon that happens near a black hole. To get a feel for it, head to the wall of mirrors in the Sky Pavilion. The reflection of your body will look long and skinny, like a strand of spaghetti. That's what you would really look like if you got too close to the gravity of a black hole. We *don't* recommend trying the real thing!

AMERICAN GIRL PLACE

Mirroring the expansion of the country it chronicles, the American Girls enterprise has expanded by leaps and bounds. This new three-level store, the first of its kind, is a destination for any girl who loves the American Girls, and many a young lady dresses up and brings her doll along to share the experience.

At the heart of American Girls is an immensely popular series of books about six girls (Felicity, Josefina, Kirsten, Addy, Samantha, and Molly) living in different places and eras of American history, from Colonial Williamsburg to World War II. While revealing nitty-gritty details about growing up during that time, the stories go beyond simple history lessons, enabling young readers to discover similarities between their own lives and the lives of these strong-willed, compassionate girls.

Out of these books, a merchandising empire has grown. Each character comes as a much-coveted doll with her own wardrobe and accoutrements, which are displayed in a glass case.

HEY, KIDS! Children long ago didn't have very many material possessions of their own. Not only did most girls have only one outfit for their doll, but they had only one doll. The American Girls themselves derived pleasure from simple games and activities. See if you can follow their example and limit the number of American Girl products that you "must have." Remember that Felicity loved just going to her father's store; she didn't have to buy stuff.

Plenty of other items can be seen (and purchased) here, too. Girls can join the American Girls Club, acquire wardrobes that match their AG dolls, or thumb through books for and about today's girls.

American Girl Place is more than just an elegant, three-level store, however. It's also a place to learn about America's history. For example, dioramas for each doll are complete down to the smallest objects and change to reflect seasons and holidays. A cozy 150-seat theater presents a musical revue for children 7 and up (reservations required), featuring young girls in the roles of the six brave characters. (The revue is replaced every year or so, but the inspiration remains the same.) Their stories should help to remind your children that the American Girls are not just about buying as much as you can, but also about the importance of believing in your strengths and following your heart.

KID-FRIENDLY EATS Windows in the fancy second-floor **Cafe** overlook the historic Water Tower, and tables are set with white linen and sparkling silver. Menu items are inspired by the books' eras. Nibble on Felicity's tea sandwiches or Josefina's corn muffins. Lunch and tea are $16 each, and dinner is $18 (reservations required). For other possibilities, *see* Hancock Observatory.

KEEP IN MIND The pressure will be on to spend a lot of money here. Discuss spending limits with your kids before you make the trip, not after they've seen all the wonderful merchandise. Or encourage them to bring their own money. You might even want to discuss how much a dollar would have bought in the days of their favorite American Girls and then let them see how far a dollar will go at today's American Girl Place.

AMERICAN POLICE CENTER
AND MUSEUM

When you see a mural depicting police officers, you'll know you've found this museum, which provides an inside look at police work. The museum was founded in 1974 by Chicago policeman Joseph Pecoraro, who felt that newspaper coverage of the violent confrontation between police and Vietnam War protesters during the 1968 Democratic National Convention was biased and sought to provide a different view of the "men in blue."

Scattered all over the high-ceilinged museum, mannequins in uniforms from around the world seem to keep an eye on you, making sure you don't touch the exhibits. A replica of a communication center crackles with the real sounds of police radio, showing what it's like to ride in a police car.

One display concerns Chicago's first female officers, hired in 1913 to uphold moral values. Today's women on the force have the same responsibilities as men. Other areas show what the police are up against. Next to a replica of a beige 1928 Model T containing mannequins

HEY, KIDS!

Look at the gallows, and then check out the wooden electric chair with a metal cap. The man who invented this one in 1890 thought high voltage was a more humane way to execute prisoners than hanging. What do you think? What do your parents think?

KEEP IN MIND Even though many youngsters see troubling images on TV these days, a close-up look at some of the items on display at the museum might still be upsetting for some. On the other hand, this could be a good opportunity to talk to your children about the dangers of illegal substances and the importance of obeying laws and the rules of the road in order to avoid accidents when walking or riding a bike. The museum plans to move to a new location, so call ahead for details.

 $4 ages 12 and up,
$2.50 children 3–11

 M–F 9:30–4:30

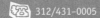 1717 S. State St.

 9 and up

312/431-0005

of the notorious couple Bonnie and Clyde stands a mannequin of a Chicago police officer. On Gangster Alley, your children can look for the movie theater seat where bank robber John Dillinger sat before he was killed by the FBI, tipped off by a lady in a red dress. The exhibit also shows photos of Al Capone and his mob, who sold illegal liquor and killed off their rivals during Prohibition, as well as some of their weapons, including a sawed-off shotgun and a machine gun. Still another display—not for the faint of heart—shows gruesome photos of crime victims, all part of the reality of police life. An open coffin is filled with illegal drugs and drug paraphernalia.

A memorial to officers killed in the line of duty contains wreaths and a police car's flashing blue light. By pressing a button, children can hear a description of the difficulties facing officers accompanied by "Amazing Grace." After a visit, your kids will indeed view officers as something other than "pigs"—what they were sometimes called during the Vietnam era.

KID-FRIENDLY EATS The museum used to be surrounded by empty buildings, which are slowly being replaced by condominiums, but as yet, no restaurants. Instead, take the opportunity to explore Chinatown's many restaurants, to the south. (Look for the Chinatown Gate, which arches over Wentworth Avenue south of Cermak Road.) The **Phoenix** (2131 S. Archer Ave., tel. 312/328–0848), which has a second-floor skyline view, is known for its dim-sum carts, which move from table to table.

ART INSTITUTE OF CHICAGO

Art might never intimidate your children again after they visit the Art Institute, a pioneer in children's art programs. Start at the Kraft Education Center, where the exhibit Telling Images: Stories in Art displays six works from different cultures and periods, as well as hands-on activities that help kids understand them. (The exhibit was designed by architect Stanley Tigerman, with input from some playful and inventive youngsters.) For example, kids can look at a montage by Martina Lopez, who used a computer to superimpose old family photographs on a mural landscape, and then have fun placing magnetized photographs on another landscape. They can push a button to hear about a 16th-century Indian Vishnu statue; try a computer game about people in the painting *Train Station,* which illustrates the South's segregation laws; or play with puppets depicting characters in the painting *St. George Killing the Dragon.*

Also in the Kraft Center, free weekend artist demonstrations might teach about printmaking, drawing from a model, or other techniques. At drop-in workshops, they might create a collage,

HEY, KIDS! Ask your parents to take you to see the collection of over 700 colorful glass paperweights on display. One of the things that's so amazing about them is that they all belonged to one person, who donated them to the museum. How do they compare with objects you collect? If you ever collect that many beautiful objects, would you display them somewhere where everyone could see them?

Michigan Ave. at Adams St.

 $8 adults, $5 students 6 and up, T free

M and W–F 10:30–4:30, T 10:30–8, Sa 10–5, Su 12–5. Guided tours Su 1:30

 312/857–7161

4 and up

a decorated paper plate, or other art project inspired by artworks here. The center also offers storytelling, puppet shows, and dance programs, and has a cozy reading room. Changing exhibits in a gallery here display original illustrations from children's books, ranging from beautiful fairy-tale paintings to cartoonlike drawings of famous artists.

To best view the "adult" galleries, take a guided or self-guided tour, the latter thanks to free, lively guidebooks. One concerns portraits from various cultures and eras, while another, called "On Guard!", covers the popular Art of Arms and Armor gallery. Brochures reveal interesting facts and ask children questions about artworks. The Ancient Art gallery also appeals to kids, who can use a computerized multimedia guide called "Cleopatra." The Thorne Rooms' miniature interiors show where everyone from kings to early Americans lived.

KID-FRIENDLY EATS The museum's **Court Cafeteria** has pizza, hot dogs, and macaroni. The **Garden Restaurant,** open in the summer, offers more sophisticated food that older children might enjoy. The children's menu at **Bennigan's** (150 S. Michigan Ave., tel. 312/427–0577) includes a choice of chicken fingers, a hot dog, macaroni and cheese, or a cheeseburger, all served with fries.

KEEP IN MIND If you and your family want to explore the museum a little bit more, buy a copy of the lively book *Behind the Lions: A Family Guide to the Art Institute of Chicago*, available at the museum store. (The title refers to the two lion sculptures at the entrance to the museum.) The book discusses approximately 60 artworks, includes color photographs, and contains instructions for art projects that children can make with simple items found around the house.

BALZEKAS MUSEUM OF
LITHUANIAN CULTURE

Located in Marquette Park, a neighborhood of many Lithuanians and other ethnic groups, this museum was created in 1966 by Stanley Balzeka to showcase his collection of Lithuanian artifacts. Today the museum, housed in a former hospital, has a main exhibit, a children's museum, space for temporary exhibits, and a research and reference library. It's a low-key place without high-powered activities, but with a little help from you, your kids can learn a little about Lithuania.

The main exhibit, Lithuania Through the Ages, is a hands-off space with most objects in glass cases. Still, many items are fascinating, including Neolithic arrowheads (15,000–6000 BC) and various ax heads (2000 BC–900 AD). Several cases contain objects made from amber. Ranging in color from pale yellow to reddish, amber is actually fossilized resin that oozed from ancient pine trees. Amber objects here include jewelry, combs, and carved pipes as well as pieces with insects caught inside long ago. Your children can also examine a suit of armor as well as spearheads used by Mindaugas, the country's first great ruler.

HEY, KIDS!

Lithuanians once believed people were influenced by the day they were born. Sunday's babies were clever, happy, and rich; Monday's were sad but successful; Tuesday's were musical; Wednesday's were lazy and good-natured; Thursday's were fat and amiable; Friday's were thin and attractive; and Saturday's liked cleanliness. How about you?

KEEP IN MIND
Most children don't know where Lithuania is, so start by pointing it out on a map—on the Baltic Sea, northeast of Poland, and west of Russia. Although the museum's Lithuanian exhibits will teach you something about the Baltic republic, another of the museum's aims is to give you a chance to reflect on your own heritage. That's why the children's museum has "Immigrant History" in its title. So take this opportunity to talk with your children about their ancestors and how your family's past lives on.

The Women's Guild Room contains mannequins dressed in colorful woven regional costumes. Handmade dolls, also dressed in regional costumes, are adorned with amber necklaces. In the Children's Museum of Immigrant History, kids can try on an amber ring and learn that Lithuanians once believed that amber had magical powers. They can play with a rag doll dressed in Lithuanian costume or with carved wooden figures in a thatch-roof house. They can also try playing a dulcimerlike instrument that wandering medieval poets used. Kids can cross a drawbridge into a castlelike room with simulated stone walls and solve a 4-foot jigsaw puzzle of a knight, stick their faces through holes in paintings of a knight and maiden in Lithuanian dress, or dress up themselves. A workshop features folk arts, where kids can make ornaments out of straw before Christmas and color eggs using onion-skin dye before Easter.

KID-FRIENDLY EATS Food in the area is the kind to please young American palates. **McDonald's** (6737 S. Pulaski Rd., tel. 773/735–6342) awaits with Happy Meals. **Alicia's Restaurant & Pancake House** (6840 S. Pulaski Rd., tel. 773/284–7570) features such breakfast fare as silver-dollar pancakes, chocolate-chip pancakes, and plain-old pancakes. Lunch choices include cheeseburgers, grilled cheese, chicken fingers, hot dogs, fried perch—all served with fries or mashed potatoes—spaghetti, and mostaccioli.

BRONZEVILLE CHILDREN'S MUSEUM

63

During the 1920s, the Bronzeville neighborhood, on Chicago's South Side between 31st and 39th streets and State Street and King Drive, was like a city within the city. Black culture, commerce, churches, and politics flourished. So it's not surprising that Peggy Montes chose the name Bronzeville for the children's black-history museum she founded in 1998. Though it currently occupies a modest space on a shopping mall's lower level, she has big plans to one day relocate it to Bronzeville, which is being revitalized. Space is limited, but the ideas of Montes, a former teacher, are not. Young visitors here can discover the important contributions of African-Americans through varied, engaging activities: make-believe play, computer games, videos and films, hands-on crafts, and a song written especially for the occasion. There is only one exhibit at a time, changing about every four months, but each one is chock-full of things to do.

During the exhibit How Blacks Built the West, young visitors could dress up and pretend to be black cowboys and cowgirls, try to spin a lasso, shop at a western-style store, or watch

HEY, KIDS! See how many famous black Americans you can name. Ask your parents to add the ones that they know. To see how much you learn from a visit to this children's museum, make one list before you go, and then make another one afterward. Bet you'll be surprised at how much you know!

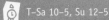

Evergreen Plaza, lower level, 95th St. and Western Ave., Evergreen Park

708/636-9504

$3 adults, $2 children 3–17

T–Sa 10–5, Su 12–5

3 and up

a short film about the amazing feats of today's black rodeo cowboys. They learned that Native Americans considered blacks their brothers and sisters and treated them cordially when they escaped from plantations. For an exhibit about botanist, agricultural chemist, and peanut expert George Washington Carver, kids could see a diorama of a peanut growing underground; listen to a talking peanut; pretend to conduct experiments with test tubes, petri dishes, and microscopes; and take a recipe for peanut butter home with them. In yet another exhibit, called African Americans in Aviation: Up and Away, kids could play a flight-simulation game, make their own plane with construction paper and Popsicle sticks, and learn about two African-American pilots who had to go to France to learn to fly. So no matter what your children's skin color, they can learn about people and exploits that deserve recognition while having lots of fun.

KID-FRIENDLY EATS The Evergreen Plaza shopping mall has a **food court** (tel. 773/445–8900) with an abundance of choices. You can opt for deli sandwiches and salads, steaks, pizza, fried chicken, Asian dishes, ice cream, and other sweets and snacks.

KEEP IN MIND Learning about the history of black Americans doesn't have to stop after a visit to the museum. Use this as an opportunity to discuss issues of race with your children, as appropriate to their age. With younger kids, get library books about African-Americans past and present who should be better known. With older children, be prepared to discuss weightier topics, such as shameful events in our country's history or why so many textbooks over the years have failed to mention many accomplished African-Americans.

BROOKFIELD ZOO

You and your family can have an almost "you are there" experience at this 216-acre zoo, where animals live in naturalistic settings. And "there" could be anywhere on the planet. Tropic World will transport you to a rain forest where some trees are 50 feet tall and regular thunderstorms drop rain on creatures from South America, Asia, and Africa. (Don't worry; you won't get wet on the walkways overlooking them.) Take a make-believe safari through Habitat Africa's 5-acre savanna to see giraffes, zebras, and African wild dogs, or walk through a swamp with a squishy-feeling walkway to see salamanders, screech owls, and other animals of the Illinois wetlands. (Don't worry here, either; you don't need mud boots.) Journey to the west coast of South America at the Living Coast: A World of Surprising Connections, and learn about moon jellies, small sharks, and sea turtles. The recorded sounds of gurgling water and of whales and other creatures as well as beams of shifting light make you feel you're underwater. The Fragile Kingdom takes you to Africa and Asia, home to Siberian tigers, snow leopards, jaguars, and lions. At the Baboon Island display, your children can learn about the research that's going on and even help to gather some. Along the ¼-mile Salt Creek

HEY, KIDS!
Play the Quest to Save the Earth game. Labels along a path explain how to play. Choose between environmentally friendly and unfriendly actions. If you make a good choice, you advance. At the end a huge brown globe turns green if you touch it and pledge to support conservation.

KEEP IN MIND
There are over 2,600 animals at the zoo, ranging from aardvarks (like Arthur on the popular PBS show) to zebras. It's hard to see them all, especially if your child is prone to tired feet or you are prone to tired arms. Get a map when you arrive and decide with your family what everyone wants to see the most. If you just don't want to do all that walking, invest in tickets for the Motor Safari.

1st Ave. and 31st St., Brookfield

 708/485-0263

 $6 ages 12 and up, $3 children 3–11; Apr–Sept, T $4 adults, $1.50 children; Oct–Mar T and Th free; some attractions extra

 Memorial Day–Labor Day, daily 9:30–6; Sept–May, M–F 10–5, Sa–Su 10–6 (to 5 Nov–Mar)

All ages

Wilderness trail, which circles a 4-acre lake, you'll see swans and other waterfowl, turtles, frogs, and raccoons. At the lake's north end is the Dragonfly Marsh.

The popular Seven Seas Panorama presents a dolphin show daily, while at the Children's Zoo, kids can pet domesticated animals and watch them in an Animals in Action presentation, which might include a pig playing soccer, a horse jumping hurdles, a goat handling an obstacle course, or sheep demonstrating their herding skills. The Rhythm & Roots Festival, comprising music, dance, storytelling, and craft activities from cultures associated with animal exhibits, usually runs Friday–Sunday throughout the summer. The zoo also holds a Teddy Bear Picnic in August, Boo at the Zoo! for Halloween, and Holiday Magic late November–December. Whew!

KID-FRIENDLY EATS The zoo has lots of concessions and restaurants: **Cafe Olé** (Mexican), **Safari Stop Restaurant** (burgers, hot dogs, pizza, and chicken sandwiches), **Backyard Barbecue, La Gran Cocina** (South American specialties, plus a salad bar, stir-fry, and pizza), **Bocaditos** (also South American), **Tonga Hut** (fried chicken, subs), **Tropic World Refreshments, Nyani Lodge,** and the **Bear Gardens Café.** Most eateries have AniMeals—with a hot dog or hamburger, fruit, and a gift.

BUCCANEER PIRATE ADVENTURE CRUISES

Young would-be pirates don pirate hats and come aboard the *Buccaneer,* a 150-passenger cruise ship resembling a pirate vessel. The boat owes its convincing pirate feel to a Jolly Roger flying overhead, a blue and black exterior, mermaid figurehead on her bow, and trompe l'oeil gun ports and cannons painted along her sides. Some of the interior has a weathered look.

The crew is a motley group dressed in bandannas, striped T-shirts, ragged shirts, and sashes—but no eye patches, since they have to see what they're doing. The captain's clothes are more elegant, including a white shirt with ruffles and a fitted jacket. While there may be a saber or two and a little pirate talk at boarding time, all that gets put aside when it's time to operate the ship.

Leaving from a dock on the Chicago River across from the Merchandise Mart, the ship motors east through the locks, where youthful pirates get a lesson in how the gates are closed and the water level raised so the boat can pass from the river to higher Lake Michigan. The *Buccaneer*

KEEP IN MIND Explain to kids the rules of safe behavior on boats before boarding, since pirates have enough dangers to contend with. Running is not permitted, because the decks may be slippery, and there's absolutely no standing on the seats or climbing on the hand rails, as no one is supposed to be walking any planks here. Children should listen carefully to the captain when he points out where the life jackets can be found in case of an emergency.

then usually heads north past Navy Pier toward Evanston. Your children can gaze at Chicago's skyline, perhaps dreaming of all the loot that could be plundered there. Or they might be too busy watching a pirate magician perform tricks and make balloon sculptures like swords, which might come in handy if the enemy appears. Since piracy can make you thirsty, budding buccaneers get a soft drink without having to fight for it.

When the weather is nice, the sides of the ship are open during the 1½-hour cruise, but a transparent protective curtain can be closed when the elements dictate, so it's not too much of an adventure. As the *Buccaneer* returns to shore, young pirates receive diplomas certifying that they have completed and survived the excursion and that they have performed all their duties. Signing the certificate and swearing to live by the pirate's code gives them the right to call themselves scoundrels.

KID-FRIENDLY EATS California Pizza Kitchen (414 N. Orleans St., tel. 312/222–9030), part of a national chain, brings multiculturalism to pizza. You can order tandoori chicken pizza, tostada pizza, or Thai or Caribbean pizza, but you can also get a plain cheese or pepperoni pizza, a surer bet for kids. Top it off with a hot fudge sundae for dessert.

CALDWELL WOODS

Native American trails once crossed this area, but in 1829 Billy Caldwell, chief of the Ottawa, Chippewa, and Potowatomi nations, helped negotiate a treaty between the Native Americans and the U.S. government. The tribes agreed to leave the region and move on to lands west of the Mississippi. To thank him for his efforts, the U.S. government granted Caldwell the land that now bears his name and belongs to the Cook County Forest Preserve. Caldwell Woods provides recreation in all seasons. Paths for walking in the woods and along the North Branch of the Chicago River lure families on pleasant spring and fall days. The diverse landscape includes patches of prairie with grasses 6 feet tall, wetlands, and savanna where wildflowers and grasses grow in between scattered trees. There is even room for picnic tables.

In summer, the Whealan Aquatic Center offers something for everyone. Serious swimmers find lanes for doing laps. Girls (and boys) who just want to have fun enjoy a long slide that zigs and zags and then zigzags again before plunging into the water. Youngsters frolic in a play area that looks like a house on stilts with water gushing over it and out of spouts

KEEP IN MIND Since the aquatic center is free, on very nice summer days the pool has been known to reach its maximum capacity, after which no one else is allowed to enter. The best way to avoid crowds *and* disappointment is to come early.

HEY, KIDS! You'll have a happier, and maybe even a healthier, time if you follow the safety and courtesy rules at the facilities here. Remember that no running is allowed at the pool and that you have to stand in line and wait your turn at all slides—both at the pool in summer and at the toboggan chute in winter.

 6200 W. Devon Ave.

 773/775–1666 aquatic center, 773/631–7657 toboggan slide

 Free; toboggans $3 per hour, chute pass $1 per day

 Daily sunrise–sunset; aquatic center mid-June–Labor Day, daily 12–7:30

All ages

around it. Wee ones like a pool that's just their size, with a minislide and small sprays of water shooting into the air. An area filled with sand is nearby. And for those who want to relax, there's a grassy area for sunbathing.

Come winter, your children may want to rent a toboggan or bring their own to use on slides constructed from snow and ice. Or they might want to bring a sled or other slippery object to slide down the hills. There's also an outdoor ice-skating rink. It's a far cry from the forest preserve the Native Americans left behind.

KID-FRIENDLY EATS The pool has a **concession stand** with tables shaded by umbrellas. Another option is **Superdawg Drive-In** (6363 N. Milwaukee Ave., tel. 773/763–0660), which is known not only for hot dogs but also for its giant statues of hot dogs dressed as humans standing on the roof.

CHICAGO BOTANIC GARDEN

These gardens may be "formal," but children don't mind; for them, a visit here is informal and fun. They can discover countless plants—including 5,000 roses—throughout the growing season. Just call or stop at the Gateway Center to find out what's blooming, and pick up a chart of the best viewing times for each area.

Begin in the Fruit and Vegetable Garden, where beds and orchards grow with good things to eat, an eye-opener for children who think produce grows in plastic at the supermarket. They can also see a beehive in action and learn about honey-making and pollination. If your kids are drawn to water, they'll enjoy walking to the top of the Waterfall Garden and watching water cascade down the hillside. If they want to get wet themselves, they'll like the fountain in the Circle Garden, where water creates 8-foot-tall arches to walk under.

The garden is even worth visiting in winter, since greenhouses, filled with plants from habitats ranging from rain forest to desert, are always warm. Your kids can look for a Venus flytrap,

HEY, KIDS! Cross the bridge that zigzags across the Japanese Garden, making sure to pay attention to where you're going. (The cement bridge has no railings, and walking straight will land you in the water.) According to the Japanese, traversing this kind of bridge is a good way to lose any evil spirits who may be following you because they can only walk in straight lines. It doesn't work on parents, though.

Lake Cook Rd. (½ mi east of
Edens Expressway), Glencoe

847/835–5440

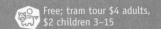
Free; tram tour $4 adults,
$2 children 3–15

Daily 8–sunset

3 and up

which catches insects and makes a meal of them, and all sorts of animal-shape topiaries, including a donkey, an orangutan, a toucan in a tree, and a towering dinosaur. Another greenhouse has food trees, such as banana and coffee plants. On a touch table, children can feel the soft and furry leaves of the panda bear plant and the smooth ones of the aloe vera. The Japanese Garden has pruned trees and stone lanterns shaped to catch the snow.

Other occasions to visit the botanical garden bloom only on selected days. Some, like the arts and crafts activities held on many weekends, are free, whereas others charge fees. In the Pill Bug Derby, a family program, children receive bugs, learn about their behaviors, and take home a bag-terrarium habitat. Day camps, a kids' gardening club, family garden picnics, sleepovers, Teddy Bear Teas, and holiday workshops dot a calendar that's always growing something fun.

KEEP IN MIND
The Chicago Botanic Garden covers 385 acres, so you'll have to plan out an itinerary that's manageable. Get a map from the information desk to pick out the gardens your family wants to visit, or take a tram tour. You can cover more ground on a tour, you won't get tired, and the kids will probably be able to spot more ducks and geese than you would on foot.

KID-FRIENDLY EATS
The **Food for Thought Cafe** (Gateway Center, tel. 847/835–3040) offers soups, gourmet salads, and sandwiches, but never fear: A "Young Set" menu features peanut butter and jelly and turkey sandwiches, hot dogs, and chicken nuggets. The café is open year-round, but in summer, you can sit on a pleasant patio overlooking water. There are more outdoor tables adjacent to the Rose Garden, where you can buy sandwiches and drinks, and in other garden areas for those who bring a picnic.

CHICAGO CHILDREN'S MUSEUM

Hip, hip hooray! This is one of Chicago's best places to play. Three floors of hands-on exhibits turn doing into believing and teach kids about the world, themselves, and others. To plan your day, get a "Guest Guide" at the admissions desk. Your first stop, however, will be obvious. Just inside waits a three-story schooner similar to ones that once sailed Lake Michigan. Children love to climb the rope ladder to the deck, carefully pick their way across a rope bridge to the gangplank, and slide down to the lower level, where there are fish like those that call the lake home. Adults are welcome aboard, too.

The most awesome exhibits are in the 50-foot towers. In one, kids use their imagination and knowledge of aerodynamics to make airplanes, send them to the tower's top on a conveyor belt, and launch them to see if they soar or plummet. In the other, children don raincoats at the Waterways exhibit, manipulate levers, and send water through brightly colored pipes, over waterwheels, and along streams waiting to be dammed. If everyone joins forces and pumps hard enough, water will shoot 50 feet in the air.

HEY, KIDS!

Twenty-seven benches created by artists are scattered throughout the museum. To find the one that makes music when you sit on it, pretend to be Goldilocks. You'll probably have to sit on a lot of benches that are "too quiet" before you find the one that's "just right."

KEEP IN MIND Once you get here, which can be a small adventure in itself (*see* Transportation *in* the Navy Pier), there are enough exhibits and activities to fill up a whole day, but you'll want to pace yourself to avoid over-tired kids. Alternate between active and quiet activities, and take a break for a snack or lunch. If you're lucky, by the end of the day your children will actually be ready to leave the museum and return to reality.

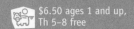
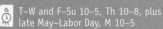

When it's time to engage the mind instead of the muscles, head to Face to Face: Dealing with Prejudice and Discrimination, on the third floor. Older children stand mesmerized in front of a video of Chicago children talking about being excluded or called names. In Dinosaur Expedition, kids pretend to be paleontologists and dig for dinosaur bones.

Two early childhood exhibits protect little ones from the hubbub. Preschoolers find a city their own size in the third-floor PlayMaze, where they pretend to be grown-up bus drivers, bakers, passengers, or customers. In the adjacent Treehouse Trails, toddlers who like the great outdoors can find shelter in a log cabin or a tree house.

Creativity is given free reign in the Kraft Artabounds Studio, on the lower level, where drop-in workshops are inspired by museum exhibits, a holiday, or other special event. Temporary exhibits are installed regularly and special activities are added often.

KID-FRIENDLY EATS Navy Pier has many eateries (for another, *see* the Navy Pier). Dimly lit, out-of-this-world **McDonald's** (tel. 312/832–1640) has occasional laser-light shows. The **Food Court** offers Chinese, Greek, and Italian fare. In the beautiful six-story, glass-domed **Crystal Gardens,** a tropical spot with burbling fountains, you can eat food you've brought from home or purchased here. The **Wave Runner Bar & Grill** (tel. 312/644–7482) has sandwiches and salads.

CHICAGO CULTURAL CENTER

When this cultural center was built in 1897, it was called the "People's Palace" because the beautiful block-long building—whose exterior was inspired by Greek and Roman architecture and whose interior was influenced by Italian Renaissance palaces—was funded by the city so that everyone could enjoy the arts free of charge. Many of the spaces on its five floors are worth visiting just to see the splendid ornamentation, including marble, polished brass, stained glass, colored stone, and mother-of-pearl mosaics. Nowadays the center is alive with many styles of music, theater, and dance—all free.

In addition to adult programs, offered daily, the center puts on children's programs on Saturday (sometimes Sunday) in the late morning and early afternoon during the school year and on occasional weekdays in summer. The Young People's Concerts present music from many cultures. One presentation might showcase rhythm instruments from Africa, India, South America, and the Caribbean, whereas in another program musicians might play folk or classical music or improvise on handmade instruments in the guitar family. Other events could

HEY, KIDS! Ask for a free copy of "A Young Person's Guide to the Cultural Center," which has lots of interesting information about the center and games to play, too. With guide in hand, look for the beautiful stained-glass domed ceiling of Preston Bradley Hall and the ceiling in the Grand Army of the Republic Rotunda, encrusted with interesting designs. The booklet challenges you to find designs, precious materials, and quotations in the interior ornamentation and to discover architectural elements.

include a performance and theater games by Redmoon Theater, known for its gigantic papier-mâché puppets and stilt-walkers; weird science demonstrations; a theater piece about an inner-city, African-American Rapunzel; a visit by staff members of the Lincoln Park Zoo, who may bring an armadillo, a rooster, or a snake; comedy improv games; and workshops on making kites, puppets, masks, and arts and crafts from many cultures. During the holiday season, programs for all ages are inspired by Christmas, Hanukkah, and Kwanza and include performances and hands-on workshops.

There is seldom a dull moment at the Chicago Cultural Center, which also houses the Museum of Broadcast Communications (*see below*). Your children can become familiar with many genres of the performing arts and with the artists themselves—and, in the process, may discover their own creative abilities, too.

KID-FRIENDLY EATS The cultural center has a **Corner Bakery** (tel. 312/201–0805), one in a chain of restaurants found around the city and the suburbs. It serves appetizing sandwiches, some on baguettes; salads; and desserts, including fudge brownies and raspberry bars.

KEEP IN MIND The cultural center hosts not only performing arts programs but also the visual arts: about a half-dozen temporary exhibits at a time. The artworks generally represent painting, photography, or sculpture but have also included abstract collages by a 92-year-old, visually impaired retired physician; quilt art that included painted images and handwritten texts; and carved wooden animals by a Japanese folk artist. So while you're here, take a walk around to see what catches your and your children's interest.

CHICAGO DUCK TOURS

56

A great way to see the city and be sure that you're noticed, too, is to take a tour on a cumbersome, open-air vehicle known as a Duck, so dubbed because its code name during World War II was DUKW. These vehicles may look like ugly ducklings, but don't let appearances fool you; they're very practical. Not only do they maneuver on land, but they float in the water as well. Their amphibious nature made them instrumental in taking soldiers and supplies ashore during the D-Day invasion of Normandy. Today's Duck can take your family on an approximately 90-minute tour of Chicago that you'll definitely remember.

The driver describes the city's sights and tries to get a few laughs as he drives through River North and along Michigan Avenue. Along the way you'll pass such government buildings as the James R. Thompson Center, which looks something like a spaceship. (Notice the sculpture by Jean Dubuffet in front, called *Monument to a Standing Beast*.) You'll see City Hall; Marshall Field's; and the two big lion sculptures perched outside the entrance to the Art Institute. But the best is yet to come.

KEEP IN MIND Ducks fill up quickly because they seat only 28, so reserve as many as three days in advance, if possible. Another good pre-trip idea is to reassure your children that though the Duck will drive into the water, it really won't sink to the bottom of Lake Michigan. Really!

HEY, KIDS! Listen for the wheels retracting as the Duck goes gently into the water. You probably won't get wet (and if you do, it'll likely be only a tiny bit), but wear some clothes that dry quickly just in case. You can also ask the driver to tell you the name of your particular Duck. It could be Huey, Louie, Dewey, Mallard, or Disco. (And if you don't know who Disco Duck is, ask your parents.)

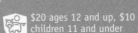 Quack Shack in parking lot of Rock 'n Roll McDonald's, Clark and Ontario Sts.

 312/461–1133

 $20 ages 12 and up, $10 children 11 and under

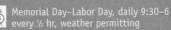 Memorial Day–Labor Day, daily 9:30–6 every ½ hr, weather permitting

All ages

At Burnham Harbor the Duck heads down a steep ramp into Lake Michigan. Trust is of the essence. It's hard to believe that the tanklike vehicle can float, but rest assured it really does. In fact, the cruise part of the tour lasts about 35 minutes. And, by the way, the driver is certified by the Coast Guard.

Back on land, the Duck cruises past the oceanarium at the John G. Shedd Aquarium, with its rounded glass windows overlooking the lake, and Buckingham Fountain, built in 1927 to look like one at Versailles—but twice as big. Its main jet of water shoots 135 feet up. And speaking of heights, you'll also pass the John Hancock Center, Chicago's third-tallest building. Okay, so you don't get a true bird's-eye view of the city, but a Duck's-eye view is still pretty remarkable.

KID-FRIENDLY EATS The nearest eatery is **Rock 'n Roll McDonald's** (600 N. Clark St., tel. 312/664–7940), from whose parking lot the Ducks depart. The Happy Meals are standard, but the decor is anything but. Large portraits of Elvis Presley, James Dean, and the Beatles adorn the exterior, and the interior is full of fabulous '50s and '60s memorabilia. Prices are slightly higher than at conventional McDonald's. For another local eatery that takes you back, *see* Ed Debevic's Short Order Deluxe.

CHICAGO HISTORICAL SOCIETY

ounded in 1856, the society is the city's oldest cultural institution, though its museum opened later. (It moved to this brick Georgian building in 1932.) But despite its serious-sounding pedigree, it has plenty to interest children. Costumed characters representing well-known historical figures give 20-minute performances in galleries; temporary exhibits feature hands-on activities; special programs take place year-round; and even permanent exhibits, especially on the first floor, are child-friendly. In fact, the Hands-On History Gallery was created for kids.

Here youngsters can pretend to be part of the city's past. They can play with paraphernalia fur traders once used and feel different animal pelts. If their legs are long enough, they can climb onto an old-fashioned high-wheeler bicycle. They can try on shirt collars and cuffs or button shoes using a buttonhook. In a corner exhibit about old-fashioned radio programs, they can create sound effects with simple items, such as coconut shells for the clip-clop of horses' hooves and a sheet of metal that, when rattled, resembles a storm.

KID-FRIENDLY EATS The museum restaurant, called **Big Shoulders** (tel. 312/587–7766) after poet Carl Sandburg's description of Chicago as the "City of the Big Shoulders," is a two-story glassed-in space with an outdoor patio. Its menu for little ones includes a grilled-cheese sandwich on millet bread served with roasted potatoes; a peanut butter and jelly sandwich, also on millet bread, with fresh fruit; hamburgers; and pasta.

Clark St. and North Ave.

 312/642-4600

$5 adults, $3 youths 13–22,
$1 children 6–12, M free

M–Sa 9:30–4:30, Su 12–5

4 and up

The Illinois Pioneer Life Galleries, also on the first floor, present life circa 1818–1850. There are places for spinning and weaving, candle-making, blacksmithing, and printing, and people wearing pioneer clothes demonstrate crafts on weekends. Your children can look at old-fashioned instruments and guess what a niddy noddy and a sausage gun were used for. (They measure yarn and shoot meat into sausage casing, respectively.)

In the Chicago History Galleries children can peer into dioramas depicting city history. A film on the Great Chicago Fire of 1871 shows how the city was destroyed and rebuilt. (No one blames Mrs. O'Leary's cow anymore.) One of the most impressive objects in these galleries is the *Pioneer,* a real locomotive from the mid-1800s. Your kids can climb into the cab and learn how the engineer stopped the train (by putting it in reverse, since it didn't have brakes). And then they'll go full steam ahead once again, learning about Chicago's past by reliving it themselves.

HEY, KIDS! Check out the objects that decorate the walls of the museum's lobby. See if you can find a toy truck and sand loader, some juggling equipment, and bottles of Hines Root Beer and the fruit drink Tango-La, both popular beverages in the Chicago of the 1930s.

KEEP IN MIND The film of the Chicago Fire is very impressive, but it might be too frightening for some children. Naturally, the subject matter is disturbing, underscored by a soundtrack that includes the crackling of flames and the shouts of people. Children 6 and up can perhaps handle it, but parents should decide if it's appropriate for a particular child.

CHICAGO MERCANTILE EXCHANGE

N either your child nor you needs to know what sorghum futures are to make a trip to the fourth-floor visitor center here worthwhile. From it, you can see fast and furious trading on the Chicago Mercantile Exchange, which looks like what happens in a preschool class when the teacher leaves the room. Traders wearing bright-color jackets stand in pits, where they shout, make faces, and wave their arms frenetically. They are all busy trying to buy or sell agricultural products—maybe live cattle, boneless beef, hog bellies, or even dried cocoons—that will be delivered in the future. Luckily, interactive computer screens help you all make sense of the apparent nonsense, explaining what's happening using animated characters, photographs of people working on the exchange, and a sense of humor.

The screaming and yelling you hear is called the "open outcry." It's a kind of auction in which one person calls out prices and others shout back that they want to buy. No wonder everyone looks so stressed. Since it's hard to be heard above the crowd, traders use a kind of sign language, too. The computer program will help you decipher these hand gestures—

KEEP IN MIND If your child enjoys the mercantile exchange, head up to the eighth floor to see more frantic behavior at the International Monetary Market, where foreign currency is traded. The visitor center here is open Monday through Friday 7:15–2.

KID-FRIENDLY EATS On the exchange's first floor, the **Wall Street Deli** (tel. 312/993–3500) has soups, sandwiches, and salads. Choices in the Presidential Towers (555 W. Madison St.) include **Bennigan's** (tel. 312/902–2500); **Cafe Italia** and **La Marguerita** (tel. 312/902–4600 for both), Italian and Mexican, respectively; **McDonald's** (tel. 312/902–2600); and **Pago Pago** (tel. 312/876–1500), serving Chinese food plus cheeseburgers. In nice weather, follow the traders outside, and get the specialty of the truck—perhaps "jerk" chicken, pizza, pasta, sandwiches, or burritos.

which ones mean buy and sell and which ones tell how much to buy and for what price. Kids can even play a game to see if they've learned them correctly. The people in the pit better have, because that's not the place to make mistakes.

Fashion-conscious teens can discover the key to the wardrobe code: Members of the exchange wear red jackets, whereas the people who report the price and quantity of a trade wear blue. Phone clerks, who use hand signals and written notes to communicate between traders and people on the phones, wear gold coats. The clerks wearing green coats with black badges help resolve discrepancies between buyers and sellers. Once your children have soaked up all this background information, have them look back down on the floor. They may find they understand the method to the traders' seeming madness after all.

HEY, KIDS! Children always want to know if the traders are rich. The answer is that it's hard to generalize about traders. Some are rich and some aren't. Some had other professions and needed a change of pace. Some are 25 years old; some are 75. The one thing they seem to have in common is that they wouldn't be happy sitting still—and quiet—in an office. Can you picture yourself as a trader?

CHICAGO MUSIC MART AT
DEPAUL CENTER

For almost 75 years, several blocks along South Wabash Avenue were known as "music row" because so many music manufacturers and shops were located there, drawing customers from all over the United States. In the 1960s, competition from suburban shopping malls put many businesses out of business. Then in 1993, a renovated historic landmark christened the Chicago Music Mart opened, and the concept of a one-stop place for musicians to shop and meet was reborn.

The mart has an atrium, mahogany storefronts, terrazzo flooring with inlaid marble accents, Prairie-style stenciling, and music for the ears. Any child who is a musician, wants to be a musician, wants to know about musicians, or just likes to listen to music will find the Music Mart a perfect place to explore. It's filled with all sorts of music-related stores, including ones carrying stringed instruments, percussion instruments, or pianos; a shop that focuses on ways to make music electronically; and CD and tape stores galore. And kids are always welcome to try the instruments.

KEEP IN MIND After listening to others and experimenting themselves, children are often inspired to start playing, and many stores here do more than sell instruments, adding rentals and lessons to their repertoire. Tiny fingers can tickle the synthetic ivories at American Music World (tel. 312/786–9600), offering acoustic and digital pianos, organs, and less-expensive keyboards. The Chicago Band & Orchestra Co. (tel. 312/341–0102) carries stringed and wind instruments in children's sizes, with three-month rentals running $58–$99. If your kids' commitment isn't strong, opt for the $3 wooden egg shaker.

Children can also hear what music sounds like when you're willing to practice a lot. A program called Tunes at Noon presents free concerts, usually held on a stage indoors, where there is seating. During the summer months, weather permitting, they move outdoors, and people sit in seats around the garden or stand. Concerts range from ones by high school and elementary school bands and choral groups to those featuring instrumental music from the Andes, jazz, blues, rock 'n' roll, Latin, big band, and classical—even dance performances. Each day is different. Though there are no concerts on Saturday, it's usually possible to hear the Classical Symphony Orchestra and the Protégé Philharmonic, which are housed in the mart, rehearsing on stage from 9 to 12:30 and 2 to 5. If your children weren't musicians before coming to the mart, it might inspire them to take up instruments or at least understand music better.

HEY, KIDS! There are many ways to make music, and you can sample a lot of them by visiting stores and trying instruments. Think about which you like best and why. Do you like the way it sounds, looks, or feels, or do you enjoy it because you blow into, pluck, or beat it? Do you want to play by yourself or in a band or orchestra? If you do decide to take up an instrument, remember that practice makes perfect.

KID-FRIENDLY EATS There are several restaurants in the Music Mart. Thai food is the specialty at **My Thai** (tel. 312/986–0999), where kids might like satay, egg rolls, chicken with rice, or just some noodles. **Sbarro** (tel. 312/663–1070), part of a chain, offers about a half-dozen kinds of pizza. The menu at the **Wall Street Deli** (tel. 312/913–0870) includes club, tuna, roast beef, and ham sandwiches; wraps, including a vegetable version; and one food that almost any kid will eat: potato chips.

CHICAGO PLAYWORKS

Playworks—whose full name is actually Chicago Playworks for Families and Young Audiences—has many reasons to be proud. Founded in 1925 as the Goodman Children's Theatre, which later became part of DePaul University, it's Chicago's longest continuously running children's theater as well as one of the first important children's theaters in the United States. Throughout the years it has garnered much praise and many awards for excellence, and current productions, directed by professionals but performed by the remarkably talented students in DePaul's Theatre School, continue to be outstanding. Plays range from traditional fairy tales to "today plays," which deal with contemporary social issues.

The theme for one season was "The American Experience in the 20th Century: Dreams Denied and Delayed, Lost and Found." The schedule included one play about two young slaves who travel the Underground Railroad to freedom, and another about children who worked 14-hour days in turn-of-the-20th-century Philadelphia textile mills and about Mother Jones, who led them on a protest march to champion their rights.

HEY, KIDS!

After some of the performances, you can join in an ice-cream social with members of the cast. This is a great opportunity not only to enjoy a yummy treat but also to talk with actors about the play. Ask a parent to find out the details by calling the theater.

KEEP IN MIND

Not all plays are appropriate for all ages, and you can't always judge what a production will be like by its name. It's best to inquire about the play beforehand so you can decide if it's right for your child. One or two performances of each production are interpreted in American Sign Language.

You can expect the costumes and stage design to be as elaborate and inventive as the plays themselves. For example, in a recent production of *Peter Pan*, not a word of the original script was changed, and yet the play was set in '90s Chicago. Some characters were dressed in grunge and rode skateboards, while others sported black leather; but Peter and friends still flew through the air. Not only did the play still make sense but the wonder of the experience remained intact as well.

Other Playworks presentations have included *This Is Not a Pipe Dream,* about the childhood of surrealist artist René Magritte, complete with striking visual images that recall his art, and *The Yellow Boat,* about a young boy who developed AIDS from a blood transfusion and found solace in art. The subject may sound morbid, but in fact it was a celebration of the joy of his life. For those not inclined to new dramas, there are also plenty of fairy tales with happy endings.

KID-FRIENDLY EATS Artists Cafe (412 S. Michigan Ave., tel. 312/939–7855) serves simple favorites and has outdoor seating. **Standing Room Only Chicago** (610 S. Dearborn St., tel. 312/360–1776) has burgers alongside healthier choices. Eat outside or in, where sports memorabilia includes 15 feet of wall from the old Chicago Stadium. **Edwardo's** (521 S. Dearborn St., tel. 312/939–3366) is part of a chain known for stuffed and deep-dish pizzas. *See* Rosenbaum ARTiFACT Center for more ideas.

CHICAGO TRIBUNE FREEDOM CENTER

For a behind-the-scenes look at the making of newspapers, take a tour of the Freedom Center, where the *Chicago Tribune* is printed (reservations required). Your children will come away with an increased understanding of and respect for the press and the presses.

A visit begins with a short film that depicts the newspaper's editorial offices in Michigan Avenue's Tribune Tower and includes interviews with some of its journalists. You'll also see a demonstration of how full-color pages are created, the result of only four colors—always the same four colors—printed one on top of the other: first blue, then red, next yellow, and finally black. The real action begins afterward, however, when you actually get to go see the presses rolling. You'll get to watch as sections with feature stories are printed. Hard news isn't printed until about midnight.

Rolls of blank paper, each weighing 2,000 pounds, travel along automatically on little carts. About 600 rolls are used each day, 1,000 for the Sunday edition. (Your family will also see

HEY, KIDS! If you're interested in becoming a journalist, listen carefully to the advice given by *Chicago Tribune* journalists in the introductory film. Write as much as you can as often as you can, and seek experience through your school newspaper. Computer skills are a must, since journalists use them to write their articles. And be prepared for some hard work just to get a job in journalism. More people want to enter the profession than there are positions.

an area where about 25,000 rolls of newsprint are stacked nine rolls high upon arrival from Canada and then moved around by a crane that can lift eight rolls at once with a vacuum system.) The odor of soy-based ink hangs in the air while paper whirs past on the presses at 25 miles an hour. In all, 10 presses each turn out 1,000 copies (averaging 64 pages each) a minute.

On another floor you and your kids can watch as different sections of the newspaper are assembled and bundled. The room resembles a theme park. All sorts of contraptions chug along and move up and down like mini–roller coasters, carrying papers from one station to the next. Finally, the newspapers are ready to be taken to the trucks that will distribute them throughout the city and beyond—maybe even to your family's doorstep.

KEEP IN MIND
Make sure your kids take a close look at a copy of the newspaper you saw getting printed. Seeing the finished product is part of the fun. Better yet, also take some time to examine a newspaper with your children before you go. It'll probably enrich the experience even more.

KID-FRIENDLY EATS With the exception of some new apartment buildings going up, the industrial zone around the Freedom Center is quite deserted, but the **Como Inn** (546 N. Milwaukee Ave., tel. 312/421–5222) is not too far away. The big restaurant is a Chicago staple for old-fashioned Italian cuisine. You'll also find Italian food at **Scoozi!** (*see* the Peace Museum). Just look for the giant red tomato above the front door. Both restaurants are within walking distance.

CHICAGO TROLLEY CO.

One of the best ways to see Chicago and get between sights is to hop aboard a red and green trolley. Resembling old-fashioned trolleys, these modern gas-powered vehicles don't use diesel, so there are no unpleasant fumes. They have oak benches and brass rails, and the sides are open in nice weather; when it's inclement, the trolleys are closed and the temperature controlled, so it's always pleasant inside.

Trolleys keep rolling, coming by every 10–20 minutes; more are added during busy times, so waits are never long. Trolleys make the same loop, with about a dozen stops around the city, starting (arbitrarily) with the Sears Tower, followed by State Street, which offers good shopping and a look at the huge steel Picasso sculpture in front of the Daley Center. (Some people think it's a dog, others a woman's head.) Next come various museums: the Art Institute, Field Museum, John G. Shedd Aquarium, and Adler Planetarium. After a stop at the Sheraton Chicago Hotel & Towers comes one at Navy Pier and its Chicago Children's Museum. Here you can catch a trolley shuttle to either the Museum of Science and Industry or the Lincoln Park

KID-FRIENDLY EATS For good places to eat, see the suggested restaurants in the listings covering each of the sights on the tour (*above*). Also *see* Double Decker Bus Tours *and* Ed Debevic's Short Order Deluxe.

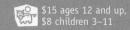

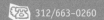
Zoo. The main trolley continues on to the Water Tower, near the John Hancock Center and more shopping; the Chicago River, site of a boat tour; the House of Blues; and the Rainforest Café. (Most of these sights are covered in separate listings.)

By staying on board for a complete loop, you can enjoy a narrated tour of about 1½ hours, as the driver interjects bits of city history, points out highlights, and throws in a few family-friendly jokes. Alternately, since passes are good all day, you can hop on and off at your leisure to visit sights, grab lunch, do some shopping, or stretch your legs. By taking multiple trolleys, you get to hear the banter of different drivers, but perhaps the biggest bonus is that if your child asks, "Are we there yet?", you can answer, "Sure, why not?" and make "there" wherever you want it to be.

KEEP IN MIND Before you get on, look at a map of the trolley route with your children so you can decide what you want to see, where you want to eat, and when to get off. You can always revise your itinerary later as interest warrants, but it often helps keep crankiness to a minimum to have a basic agreed-upon plan.

DISNEYQUEST

Disney goes high-tech at this indoor play venue, where you pay for each activity rather than a fixed admission price. Five floors are packed with interactive play areas, many employing virtual reality, that transport you and your children to places both dangerous and fanciful, around the world and beyond.

In the Explore Zone kids can hop into a raft and "ride" the rapids through a virtual jungle as they try to avoid ferocious 3-D dinosaurs and escape before a meteor crashes to earth. It's not virtual water, so be prepared to get wet. They can also fly Aladdin's magic carpet into a world of wonder or help Hercules gather lightening rods to battle Hades.

In the Score Zone children can fight villains or climb onto a giant disc to get in the middle of a slam-bam game in the Mighty Ducks Pinball Slam. The Replay Zone is the place to win tickets redeemable for prizes. In Buzz Lightyear's Astroblaster, kids ride in bumper cars and shoot balls at the other vehicles to spin them slightly out of control.

HEY, KIDS! Pay close attention when you take the Cyberlator, a newfangled elevator that takes you from the lobby up to the Venture Port, where the action begins. The ride only lasts a short time, but there's a lot going on. The ground beneath rumbles, and then you'll hear the sound of a blastoff and see lights begin to flash. You'll probably feel like you're going up very, very high. Keep your eyes open wide, and you'll see the Genie from Aladdin.

When your kids start suffering from sensory overload, head toward the Create Zone, where your little ones can flex their artistic muscles. They can design a painting by touching their fingers to the screen of the Living Easel or create a toy as Sid did in *Toy Story,* by choosing different parts from animals and humans and combining them via computer into a unique creature. For $10 they get a 3-D replica to take home. On the Magic Mirror screen, kids morph their faces, acquiring Mickey Mouse ears or other Disney character features. Save CyberSpace Mountain for last. The calm is over and the imagination goes wild as your children design their own roller coasters—with as many loops and spins as they want—and then take a virtual ride on it. They may be too breathless afterward to do anything else.

KEEP IN MIND
Since this place is operated by Disney, you can count on it being clean, safe, well-supervised, and potentially expensive. Don't let your kids get too caught up in the games that give tickets for redeemable prizes. The trinkets aren't worth the money spent (it adds up quickly), and besides, there are plenty of other activities worth exploring.

KID-FRIENDLY EATS
For snacks like cheesecake and smoothies, try the **Wonderland Cafe,** which looks like the maze that Alice encountered in her adventures. You can check out Internet sites and games and make a postcard of your DisneyQuest visit. **FoodQuest** serves more substantial favorites, such as burgers, pizza, and hot dogs in a setting that resembles an old Hollywood version of the future. The **Jekyll and Hyde Club** restaurant (43 E. Ohio St., tel. 312/644–9900) has pseudo-scary animatronic figures.

DIVERSEY MINIATURE GOLF

hy choose this course over other Chicago miniature links? Simply put, because it's one of the kindest, gentlest courses around. Many families with young children play here because it's never very crowded and you won't be pressured to play quickly by the golfers behind you, a plus when young children are just getting a grasp of the game. Another plus is the setting: a lovely tree-shaded area of Lincoln Park with a small adjacent play area. It's next to a harbor where boats are docked, and you can see the Chicago skyline in the distance. Recently renovated, the course has enough difficult obstacles to keep older children challenged and some that remain (or were made) simpler, for novices to conquer. Somehow even the littlest players manage to push the ball around a bit and get it into the hole willy nilly, to the enjoyment of all.

Despite the renovation, the obstacles aren't big and fancy, but rather small and not too intimidating. Some holes here are pretty straightforward. You might have to hit a ball through a space at the bottom of a barn or lighthouse, around an S-curve, across a bridge, or

HEY, KIDS!

Remember that doing well in miniature golf is a mixture of skill and luck. It's fun to keep score, but don't take the outcome too seriously. Even Tiger Woods loses a lot more than he wins. It's being a good sport that always makes you a winner.

KEEP IN MIND
Miniature golf does have rules, so it's best to explain them to all players before you begin. To manage your children's sometimes inevitable frustration, you might want to tailor the rules to suit. Setting a maximum number of strokes can be a blessing or a curse, depending on the child. Younger children might need a little rule-bending to enable them to get the ball in the hole before their next birthday. For older kids, it might be more important to ensure that everyone adheres to the rules, so no one feels cheated. Hopefully, the fun will outweigh any frustration.

141 W. Diversey Pkwy.

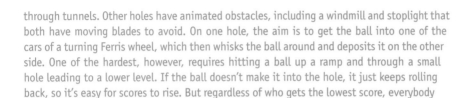 312/742-7929

$5 ages 13 and up, $4 children 12 and under

M–F 9 AM–11 PM, Sa–Su 7 AM–11 PM, weather permitting

2 and up

through tunnels. Other holes have animated obstacles, including a windmill and stoplight that both have moving blades to avoid. On one hole, the aim is to get the ball into one of the cars of a turning Ferris wheel, which then whisks the ball around and deposits it on the other side. One of the hardest, however, requires hitting a ball up a ramp and through a small hole leading to a lower level. If the ball doesn't make it into the hole, it just keeps rolling back, so it's easy for scores to rise. But regardless of who gets the lowest score, everybody wins here in an atmosphere that isn't highly competitive.

After the game, winners can celebrate their victory and high scorers can forget their defeat at the adjacent playlot. It's filled with swings, ramps, a bridge and tunnel, and a rope net shaped like a spider web ready to tangle the unsuspecting. For another diversion, kids can check out the adults honing their non-miniature golf skills at the double-decker driving range next door.

KID-FRIENDLY EATS Next to the miniature golf course is a **Subway** (248 W. Diversey Pkwy., tel. 773/281–1212) featuring sandwiches and smoothies. There are outdoor tables in the shade and lots of grassy areas to sit. For nearby restaurant choices, *see* the Lincoln Park Zoo.

DOUBLE DECKER BUS TOURS

B etter known as London icons, double-decker buses are now letting people in Chicago discover the excitement of looking down on the city. A ticket buys passage on a 90-minute narrated tour, in which the driver points out landmarks and talks about Chicago history on up to the Jordan (or should we say Sosa?) era. As with the trolley tours, however (*see* the Chicago Trolley Co.), you can also get off and on repeatedly for no extra charge, enabling your family to travel around Chicago without having to look for a parking place.

The buses stop at eight desirable locations: the Sears Tower, from whose Skydeck you can view Chicago from an even higher level; State Street and Washington Avenue, for shopping at Marshall Field's (111 N. State St.), Carson Pirie Scott (State and Madison Sts.), Old Navy (State and Washington Sts.), and Toys R Us (10 S. State St.); the Art Institute; the Museum Campus, a park area that surrounds the Field Museum, the John G. Shedd Aquarium, and the Adler Planetarium; Navy Pier, home to the Chicago Children's Museum and other attractions and restaurants; the Water Tower, a survivor of the 1871 fire where you can ride in an old-

HEY, KIDS! Looking out the window from the top deck is great, but listen to what the driver has to say, too. The narrative will teach you something about the history and architecture of Chicago. It's most interesting for kids 13 and older. If you're younger, you'll probably be more interested in just being up so high in the open air.

Eight stops (see below)

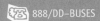 888/DD–BUSES

$12 ages 11 and up, $8 children
10 and under who take up a seat

Early Apr–late Oct, daily 9:30–5

All ages

fashioned horse-drawn carriage (Michigan Ave. and Pearson St.), visit the nearby Hancock Observatory, or shop at Water Tower Place (across the street) as well as Disney (717 N. Michigan Ave.) and Niketown (669 N. Michigan Ave.) stores; Wacker Drive and Michigan Avenue, where you'll find boat cruises; and Sammy Sosa's restaurant (opening spring 2000), an eatery dedicated to the Cubs slugger that was formerly a shrine to Michael Jordan. (See listings describing most of these sights.)

Though the fleet dates from times past, the interiors have been refurbished and the exteriors painted that recognizable bright red. Almost all the buses have open upper decks, but one has a covered top for use when the weather is bad. Still, this isn't an activity that's suggested for rainy days, no matter how much you feel like you're in London.

KID-FRIENDLY EATS See suggested restaurants in listings for the stops along the tour. At the last stop, in addition to Sammy Sosa's you can opt for the eatertainment of the **Rainforest Café** (605 N. Clark St., tel. 312/787–1501) The lavishly decorated planet-theme restaurant with an enormous green frog above its entrance offers expectable kid food with a side of environmental awareness.

KEEP IN MIND Your kids might want to run from one window to another, but explain that it's important to stay put for safety's sake. The bus does not have seat belts, and children must remain in their seats and keep their hands and arms inside the bus. You can bring strollers aboard if they fold up.

DUPAGE CHILDREN'S MUSEUM

Unbeknownst to children, there's a whole lot of learning about the world going on in this wonderful place to play. Located in the Wheaton Park District Community Center, the museum is an open, brightly lit space with areas for kids to touch everything and learn firsthand about the arts, math, and science. A new location in Naperville will be more spacious, so that some current exhibits can be enlarged and others added.

Some kids gravitate to the Construction House, where they can use saws, hammers, and other real tools on projects—from sawing wood in two to building a chair for a Beanie Baby. Parents needn't worry about safety. Tools and equipment are scaled to fit small hands, children wear safety goggles, and staff members and volunteers are on hand to help.

Others are drawn to the Physics Factory, where they can manipulate magnets or play with a weird roller coaster and a maze with a ball inside that never stops rolling. Kids can create all kinds of music at the Sound Playground or see how water works at the Water Ways

HEY, KIDS!

One of the museum's most popular areas is called Yes, I Can, where you can discover some of what it feels like to be disabled. Try to maneuver a wheelchair. It's probably not as easy as you thought. Now imagine how hard it would be if the museum wasn't handicapped accessible!

KEEP IN MIND Children have their own ways of playing at the museum. Some get caught up in one exhibit and want to stay there the whole time, whereas others want to try everything. Even if you are restless or, conversely, engrossed in something, try to follow your child's lead. Ultimately, you'll both probably enjoy the museum more that way.

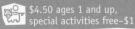

1777 S. Blanchard Rd., Wheaton (as of late 2000: 301 N. Washington St., Naperville)

630/260-9960

$4.50 ages 1 and up, special activities free-$1

T and Th-Sa 9:30-5, W 9:30-8, Su 12-5; special activities daily usually 10-12 or 1-3

18 mths-11 yrs

exhibit, where they can watch an 88-foot stream flow over waterwheels and discover what floats and what doesn't. At the No Numbers Math Station, they can explore objects with patterns and create some of their own, but don't tell them it's math. They just know it's fun.

As a preview of coming attractions at the new location, kids can already play with some expAIRiment areas, part of the AirWorks for Kids exhibit. Children will become investigators, trying to discover the properties of air and how to make it work in different ways.

A variety of special activities inspired by the exhibits are scheduled regularly. Budding artists can make works out of paper, clay, sand, or plastic forks and spoons. Little builders might create a shelter using poles, some string, and a blanket. Family workshops (registration required) include Goopy and Gushy Kidworks, featuring messy art and science projects for a child and an adult partner to share.

KID-FRIENDLY EATS Chili's (240 Danada Square W, tel. 630/690-2334) serves burgers, hot dogs, pizza, and chicken crispers. **Grady's American Grill** (301 E. Loop Rd., tel. 630/752-0311) offers similar fare along with Teddy Grahams and a balloon. The kids' menu at **Houlihan's** (321 Rice Lake Rd., tel. 630/690-5550) is a coloring book. Youngsters get a fresh fruit appetizer, entrée, drink, and ice cream. You won't starve in Naperville either, where nearby Ogden Avenue has child-friendly restaurants.

DUSABLE MUSEUM OF AFRICAN
AMERICAN HISTORY

In 1961 Margaret T. Burroughs, cofounder of the National Conference of Negro Artists, started this museum in her home, and in 1973, it moved here, to this former administration building in Washington Park. The museum's exhibits and programs explore the history of black Americans and their African origins and celebrate their culture, past and present.

One such exhibit is the re-created office of Harold Washington, Chicago's first black mayor, who died while in office. Notice the black carved wood stool, like ones given to chieftains in Ghana. (These stools are traditionally blackened when their owner dies.) You can also watch a video that highlights Washington's career.

The permanent collection has more than 10,000 pieces of African-American and African art, displayed on a rotating basis. Ask to see *Freedom Now,* by Robert Ames, in the auditorium. The 8½-foot by 10-foot wood carving depicts aspects of black history from pre-slave-trade Africa to the United States in 1963.

KID-FRIENDLY EATS The museum's location in Washington Park makes it a beautiful place for a picnic. The **CAM Food Court** (5758 S. Maryland St., tel. 773/834–8782), on the second floor of the Center for Advanced Medicine, is open weekdays 7–5. Food stations in the gray and burgundy ultramodern setting offer deli foods, pizzas, wraps, salads, stir-fries, yogurt, and smoothies. There is no problem pleasing kids at **Leona's** (1236 53rd St., tel. 773/363–2600), part of a chain, because pizza's on the menu.

740 E. 56th Pl.

 773/947–0600

 $3 ages 14 and up, $2 students 14 and up, $1 children 6–13, Su free

M–Sa 10–5, Su 12–5

Varies by exhibit

In addition, temporary exhibits are regularly displayed, remaining for about six months. Among exhibits that have really appealed to kids was Hoop History, which documented Chicago street basketball. It contained a variety of play stations, including a shooting cage and an area where visitors could get introduced the same way Bulls players are before games.

Finally, there are various programs that children might like: Celebrating the Dream and the King Day Celebration (both January); the Arts and Crafts Family Festival and the Penny Cinema, which costs 1¢ (both July); Alternative Halloween, where children dress as famous black history-makers (October); and Adorned Trees, featuring trees decorated with objects recalling black people and the places they live, and How to Celebrate Kwanza (both December). On Saturdays April through June, workshops let kids make such items as dolls, quilts, and masks. Most programs are free or carry a small charge.

KEEP IN MIND
The museum may not immediately appeal to children. To help yours get the most out of a visit, ask leading questions. Have them compare the images of African-Americans in the artworks here to those they see on TV shows and the news. Challenge your kids to figure out what various African objects were used for, since most were functional.

HEY, KIDS! You probably won't need much persuading to go visit the museum's gift shop. But this one is interesting as much for what it is as what is in it. The indoor store is a log cabin similar to one built in the 1770s by fur trader Jean-Baptiste Point du Sable, a black man credited with being Chicago's first non–Native American resident.

At ECHO—a nickname for the Eloise M. Martin Center of the Chicago Symphony Orchestra—music reverberates in the minds of young people. Though its Music Lab, where kids try instruments, is only available for groups who've reserved in advance, the A-Musing Room is the perfect place for individuals. Comprising booths with different electronic activities, it's in tune with today's video-game and computer wizards.

At first the space seems subdued. Lights are low, and carpeting keeps the noise down. But once your children get their music boxes and enter booths resembling London phone booths, the action starts. Booths are equipped with touch-screen computers ready to dispense all sorts of musical information. Plugging in a music box activates the touch screen, and the sounds of music, from classical to jazz, are at your kids' fingertips.

In the Sounds and Silence booth, experimentation reveals how vibrations make music. In Mapping and Recording, youngsters see how musical scores and street maps are similar

HEY, KIDS!
After your visit to ECHO, listen to classical music on the car radio or at home, and see if you can hear some of the elements you learned about. You may be surprised to find you enjoy the music more now that you understand it better.

KEEP IN MIND To take your child's music education further, why not subscribe to the Chicago Symphony Orchestra's regular Family Matinee series? Three concerts ($9–$21 per ticket) are given at Symphony Center (220 S. Michigan Ave.) on Saturday at 11 and 12:30 between mid-November and mid-April. Each concert includes a visual element, and each is preceded by a 45-minute lobby performance by members of the Old Town School of Folk Music. A Welcome Yule! concert always features a song written about Christmas in Chicago; a verse about current events is added annually.

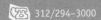

and then can record their own composition on their instrument box. In Teams, they'll learn how musicians work together and can join in as percussionists with the Chicago Symphony Orchestra. The voice of the orchestra's director, Daniel Barenboim, will tell them how well they performed. In the Links booth, they can choose a piece of music and then select objects that create a visual picture of how the music makes them feel. Their choices are assembled in a scrapbook on screen and can be compared to others made by people listening to the same music. The role of music in our everyday lives is the focus of Celebrations and Time, where the music on tap includes lullabies from around the world and party music by the Sones de Mexico Ensemble. For the grand finale, children plug their instrument boxes into the Orchestra Wall, where their melodies become part of a short symphony, and their names light up on their boxes as their compositions play.

KID-FRIENDLY EATS The **Corner Bakery** (900 N. Michigan Ave., tel. 312/573–9900) sells European-style loaves of bread and serves sandwiches and salads made with very fresh ingredients and lots of delicious desserts. Mini-sandwiches and half a pizza are available for small appetites. *See* the Art Institute of Chicago for information on other restaurants.

ED DEBEVIC'S SHORT ORDER DELUXE

One story, which may or may not be true, has it that Ed Debevic based his self-named eateries on a Talooca, Illinois, diner from the '50s and '60s (Lill's Homesick Diner, to be exact) because he was homesick for home-cooked food and feel-good times. Whether the tale is authentic or not, these raucous eateries are hardly strict interpretations of a '50s diner. Their motto could be "anything goes," and it usually does.

For starters, the focus isn't really on the food. How can it be with a noise level high enough to drown out rambunctious children? Wacky DJs play records from the era and add a few outrageous sound effects, such as a bit of snoring. One might interrupt a song to announce the make, model, and license plate of a car that's on fire in the parking lot, but it's just a practical joke and everybody knows it.

The behavior of the wait staff is just as outrageous. They dress and act the way children would if their parents allowed it, and you might have to explain to impressionable youngsters

HEY, KIDS! Break your piggy bank and bring some change. Oodles of replica candy machines dispense jaw breakers and bubble gum and lemon drops for 25¢ or so, but check with mom or dad first. There's even a booth where you can get your photograph taken, just like in the '50s. But you won't find '50s prices; it's $4 for one Polaroid shot.

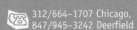 640 N. Wells St., Chicago; 660 W. Lake Cook Rd., Deerfield

312/664–1707 Chicago, 847/945–3242 Deerfield

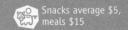 Snacks average $5, meals $15

 F–Sa 11 AM–12 AM, Su–Th 11–10

 All ages

that these so-called adults should not be considered role models. Picture, if you will, one waitress wearing an oversize balloon sculpture on her head and another with a necklace of stuffed animals, while a waiter, dressed in a Hawaiian shirt and sporting bright blue hair, dances on a counter. In fact, there is counter dancing and singing every ½ hour, complete with spotlights, colored lights, and the sparkling lights from a disco ball (so what if it's from the '70s—it just adds to the craziness). You may be treated to tap dancing, sing-alongs, or an Elvis Presley imitation by talented servers who often aspire to show business careers. In the meantime, they're happy to talk back to the customers (who expect it).

Aqua leatherette upholstery and overdone '50s and '60s paraphernalia form the backdrop. And by the way, people do eat here. The menu includes hamburgers, hot dogs, and such old-style dishes as meat loaf and pot roast.

TRANSPORTA-TION In a neighborhood where parking is practically impossible, the Chicago Ed Debevic's has its own parking lot—the way places used to in the 1950s before real estate got so expensive. Today, though, it costs $5, it's valet parking, and you can stay only as long as you are in the restaurant.

KID-FRIENDLY EATS Other area restaurants that dish out rock with the hamburger rolls include **Rock 'n Roll McDonald's** (see Chicago Duck Tours) and the **Hard Rock Cafe** (63 W. Ontario St., tel. 312/943–2252), another in the worldwide chain where loud music and rotating memorabilia rule. Lil' Rocker Meals include Jimi Tenderstix and Ain't Nothin' But a Hotdog, accompanied by french fries, apple sauce, and carrot sticks. For still more local options, see Double Decker Bus Tours.

ELI'S CHEESECAKE WORLD

Eli's cheesecakes were created as desserts for Eli's The Place for Steak in Chicago, but word spread about how tasty they are. Now they're found all over the country and as far away as Hong Kong and Iceland, giving credence to the name Eli's Cheesecake World. Almost as good as eating Eli's cheesecakes, however, is touring the bakery where they originate.

Except for the white paper cap like those worn by employees—mandatory for everyone who tours the bakery—it's hard to know what to wear. In the baking room the temperature feels tropical. Here you can taste the crust, either chocolate or shortbread, which is cooked before the batter is dropped into the pan. A conveyor belt then moves the cakes through a tunnel-shaped oven, and they are put on the bottom of a cooling rack that spirals slowly up two stories. When the cakes reach the top two hours later, they're cool enough to take out of the pan. In the background you'll hear the cling-clang of empty baking pans sliding off a conveyor belt into a container.

KEEP IN MIND The price of cheesecakes in the store at Eli's Cheesecake World is less than what you'll find elsewhere. Ones with slight imperfections are even better bargains, so why not buy two? Your family will no doubt want seconds of these seconds.

HEY, KIDS! To see who else likes Eli's cheesecake, look at the photos on the wall in the café/store. You'll see one of Jay Leno at the bakery, another of Mickey Mouse (a true cheese lover) eating a slice, one of Hillary Rodham Clinton cutting a cake that was made for her 50th birthday, and the 2,000-pound cheesecake baked for President Clinton's inauguration in Washington, D.C. Now that would be a little big even for a teenager.

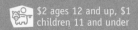
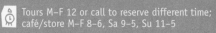

From here the cakes are frozen and then frozen some more. Whereas most of the employees wear white, some are dressed in dark parkas so they can tolerate the freezers. After a brief stint in a cool room, where the cakes are decorated by hand, they return to the freezer before a machine cuts them and puts a piece of paper between each slice, ready for some lucky buyer.

If the tour whets your family's appetite, stop at the café, which carries some 20 cheesecake flavors for sale by the slice—perhaps White Chocolate Raspberry Swirl, Oh My! Mud Pie, Peanut Butter Blast, or Toffee Talk, made with Heath Bar pieces. If you're with a group tour of 20, or if you request it, your child can decorate a slice of plain or chocolate-chip cheesecake, the company's all-time favorite flavors. Except for the noon tour, for which you can walk in, tours should be scheduled two weeks in advance.

KID-FRIENDLY EATS If you're actually hungry after your visit to Eli's Cheesecake World, there is a **McDonald's** (6400 W. Montrose Ave., Harwood Heights, tel. 708/867–1600) nearby. If you don't mind driving a bit, you can go to the **Superdawg Drive-In** (*see* Caldwell Woods) for a slice of Chicago folklore.

ESPN ZONE

B ring along lots of energy when you come to this sporting venue, because it's not just for spectators. It's for athletes big and small, too. No admission is charged to enter this two-story sports bar and entertainment center. You pay based on what you do.

The Sports Arena is the place to play, where everyone can try out their skills. You and your children can dribble and shoot baskets on a half court, scoring points based on the difficulty of the spots from which you shoot. Younger children can show off because the basket can be lowered to suit their stature. Meanwhile you can see how you measure up against the NBA players who have tested the hardwood here. If you prefer, you and your kids can pretend to be NHL players, with one of you taking shots on simulated ice while another plays goalie. Wannabe football players can see if their aim is good enough to throw the ball through moving cutouts. And X Games have a place here, too. A simulated rock-climbing wall moves down like a vertical treadmill so you can't get to the top. And don't worry: There's padding all around for those who might lose their footing.

HEY, KIDS! Check out the Zone Art displays, which have been created by local artists. One is made up of thousands of wrappers from Wrigley chewing gum that have been assembled to create a replica of the Chicago Cubs' Wrigley Field. In a piece called *Oh Say Can You Scream*, a comment on how loudly Blackhawks fans sing the national anthem, hockey sticks and pucks create an American flag. A quilt in honor of the White Sox includes—you guessed it—white socks, as well as baseball cards. How do the cards compare to ones you've collected?

Away from the heaviest action, there are lots of sports-inspired video games, but the Screening Room is the place to really be a couch potato. Here Zone Throne stations have reclining leather chairs where you can watch sporting events on a 16-foot by 13-foot screen.

Kids who feel the urge to take a break don't have to worry about missing out on the action. Even the rest rooms are equipped with television monitors so the play-by-play goes on. After all, first and foremost ESPN is a TV station.

KEEP IN MIND
Try to go at a time when there isn't a very popular sporting event scheduled to air on TV. That way your children (and you) won't get overwhelmed by overenthusiastic adult fans.

KID-FRIENDLY EATS The **Studio Grill** is decked out like the sets of ESPN shows, including "SportsCenter," "Baseball Tonight," "NBA 2Night," and "NFL Primetime." Nonreaders can still grasp the kids' menu (hamburgers, pizza, and chicken tenders) by peeking into a View-Master. When the lights dim, a sports report made for ESPN Zone is about to air on over 200 TVs. And if your children want a memento, you can take their pictures at the SportsCenter desk. Just remember to bring a camera.

FIELD MUSEUM OF NATURAL HISTORY

40

The field covered at the famous Field Museum is natural history, and the breadth of its collections is enormous. Exhibits range from the awesome to the slightly frightening to the enlightening. Descending through a dim ancient Egyptian tomb can be intimidating, but it's worth it. Mausoleums like this were called the "mansions of eternity" because the deceased who "lived" here were supposed to do so forever. The real mummies here are nothing like those that wander around in old movies, though. At the tomb's exit, your children can see how Egyptians lived and try to move a stone like the ones in the pyramids.

Dinosaurs inhabit Life Over Time. Push one button to hear the bellowing sound they might have made, another for their footsteps. If you're brave, push yet another to smell their hypothetical breath. Pause at the McDonald's Fossil Preparation Laboratory, where staff members aren't developing the McDino. (The lab is funded by the Oak Brook–based fast-food chain.) They're preparing the bones of Sue—named for the fossil's discoverer and, at 45 feet long, the largest, most complete *Tyrannosaurus rex* ever found—for display in May 2000. With

KEEP IN MIND The museum has too many interesting exhibits to be adequately covered in a day by anyone with feet. Get a map and visit the exhibits you really want to see, breaking for food every so often. At least there's now a free trolley shuttle to get you back to the parking lot.

HEY, KIDS! Look for the Living Together exhibit, which demonstrates the differences and similarities of everyday life in various cultures. A display of some 350 pairs of shoes includes silver wedding slippers from India, snowshoes worn by Eskimos, wooden shoes from the Netherlands, and a pair that belonged to Michael Jordan. They're in a glass case, so you won't be able to hold them up and compare them to your shoes. Trust us: they're bigger.

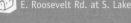
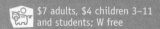

contributions from McDonald's and Walt Disney World Resort, the museum bought Sue at auction for $7.6 million, $8.4 million including commission.

Into the Wild: Animals, Trails & Tales is, as its name suggests, like traveling into the wilderness. Realistic dioramas feature animals in natural settings. Your children can push buttons to hear birdsongs or play a computer game about controlling the deer population. In a Pacific islands exhibit, your kids can experience a volcano, and in Underground Adventure, they'll encounter an animatronic crayfish, earwig, and other soil dwellers. Be prepared; they're as big as a young child. For calm, head to Families at Work: Strategies for Rearing Young, which has a childproof play area for preschoolers. Place for Wonder is another oasis of calm, where wee ones can try on Native American regalia or feel tree bark and animal scales.

KID-FRIENDLY EATS Yes, the museum does have a real **Mc-Donald's,** decorated with photographs of dinosaur skeletons and fossils and some giant murals of these extinct creatures. You can eat on an outdoor terrace when the weather is nice. A **Corner Bakery,** within a few dinosaur strides of the *Brachiosaurus* in the museum's main hall, sells mini-sandwiches, muffins, bagels and cream cheese, and even half a pizza. You can also buy box lunches and eat outside on the Museum Campus lawn.

What better way to learn about Frank Lloyd Wright's early Prairie-style architecture than to take a guided tour of the house he built for his family in 1889? Though he hadn't fully developed the style, many elements are here.

The best choice for kids is a Junior Interpreter Tour, given by young guides for young people. These focus on the life of the architect's six children and the details he included to make their home a great place to play. The tour begins with children comparing drawings of Victorian and Prairie-style houses. The Victorian is tall, wooden, and has a pointed roof. Wright's house, inspired by the Midwest landscape, is low and flat and made of stucco and bricks. Then it's time to see the house, whose first three rooms flow together with no doors to separate them.

The playroom is particularly awe-inspiring. Here a skylight brings sunshine through the 18-foot barrel-vaulted ceiling. Wright's interest in nature is visible in the leaf and tree decorations in the wooden border around the skylight and in the tulip shapes in the stained-glass windows.

HEY, KIDS! To see how Wright *really* incorporated nature in his buildings, check out the enclosed passageway between the home and the studio. Since a tree was already growing here, he simply included it in his plan. The original tree was a weeping willow, but it unfortunately suffered too much stress from the temperature difference resulting from being half indoors and half outdoors. It was replaced in the late '70s with a honey locust, which appears to be holding up.

951 Chicago Ave., Oak Park

 Standard tour $8 adults, $6 children 7–18; junior tour $1.50

708/848–1976

 Standard tour M–F 11, 1, and 3; Sa–Su 11–3:30; junior tour 4th Sa of mth at 10

 6 and up

A mural depicting "The Fisherman and the Genie," one of the Wright children's favorite stories, adorns a wall. Though built-in cabinets create plenty of storage for toys, some are just left out and around. (Some things never change.) In particular, look for the Froebel blocks, which Wright credited with shaping his architectural concepts. The keyboard of a grand piano protrudes from a wall. (Your children can find the back half sticking out on the other side of the wall by a staircase.) And the room's balcony served as either stage or gallery, depending on where the children performed.

On to the partitioned bedroom, which Wright's children shared. Though the boys slept on one side and the girls on the other, the wall wasn't high enough to prevent them from having pillow fights over the top. Perhaps your children will see that though the great architect's house is undeniably a work of art, it was also a place where kids not unlike themselves really lived.

KID-FRIENDLY EATS At **Peterson's** (715 W. Lake St., tel. 708/848–5020) you can order soup and a sandwich while your children can choose from standard kids' fare or, more likely, chicken nuggets shaped like dinosaurs. The sweetshop here serves traditional ice cream treats, but kids usually choose the Merry-Go-Round, which teams a chocolate sundae with animal cookies and a parasol.

KEEP IN MIND If Wright's own house has intrigued you, walk around the neighborhood to see other homes he designed. These are marked on a map ($3) available at the shop here. Though these houses are not open to the public, you can look at their facades to get a fuller understanding of Prairie style. The Heurtley House (318 Forest Ave.), built in 1902, is a good example of Wright's strong horizontal lines. The Frank Thomas House (210 Forest Ave.) is also typical Wright. For a fun game, ask your kids if they can pick out his houses.

GARFIELD PARK CONSERVATORY

38

Previously, this large glass-enclosed conservatory was a place to look at plants—4 indoor acres filled with them—but not to touch. All that changes in 2000, when the Elizabeth Morse Genius Children's Garden opens, not only welcoming small hands but inviting almost total body contact.

The new exhibit gives an inside look at plants and their life cycle. A giant make-believe vine beckons youngsters to crawl inside its root and make their way to a giant seed, where life begins. Handles all over the seed invite climbing. Children then move along the vine to an enormous leaf—photosynthesis in action. A large pinwheel-like sun shines above, and they can make small yellow balls of "sunshine" fall onto the leaf. The balls are absorbed and returned to the sun, where they fall again. The vine continues to the mezzanine, where a giant bee hovers above a flower. Manipulating a pulley brings the insect down to pollinate the flower, and the cycle begins again. Kids can check out a discovery area with plant books and examine a large double-coconut seed and a microscopic orchid seed.

KID-FRIENDLY EATS Often on the weekends the conservatory has a cart that sells muffins and snacks, but plans are under way to open a café on the premises. The nearest restaurant is **Wishbone** (*see* the Museum of Holography).

KEEP IN MIND The neighborhood around the conservatory isn't very safe, so you shouldn't stray far. Taking a car is your best bet. There's free parking in a lot that's safe for both you and your vehicle, so that shouldn't keep you from visiting. Good reasons to come are the flower shows: the Azalea/Camellia Show (February–March); the Pink Flamingo Show, with '50s memorabilia (early April–mid-May); the Summer Tropical Show (mid-June–early October); Chrysanthemum Flower Show (November); and the Celebration in Lights tropical salute to Santa (mid-December–mid-January).

Then put that new knowledge to work in the rest of the conservatory, where plants from around the world are labeled with interesting information. The Desert House contains cacti, which have adapted to their hot, dry climate, whereas in the Palm House, palms, ficus, and fig trees cope with excess moisture on their leaves. Kids might notice that plants growing close to the ground have big leaves (to get as much sun as possible). Children can imagine dinosaurs devouring the prehistoric plants in the Fern Room and themselves devouring the products of the Warm House's food plants, including banana and cacao trees, both integral to banana splits (cacao seeds are needed for chocolate). Your kids may not have thought about where food comes from before this, but it's amazing what planting a seed in an active mind can do.

HEY, KIDS! The Sensory Garden has plants to touch and smell as well as see. Feel the leaves of mullein, which are covered with a dense, wooly down. Touch the leaves of lamb's ear, soft as a baby's skin. Smell the lavender, garlic, chives, spearmint (like the chewing gum), thyme, and basil. Sorry, there's nothing to hear or taste here, but you might have dried thyme and basil leaves in your kitchen at home. Ask your parents if you can taste them.

GROSSE POINT LIGHTHOUSE

This lighthouse offers up a view of Lake Michigan that will be long remembered, but it's not for everyone. Any individuals who have vertigo, a fear of heights, claustrophobia, or are unsteady on their feet should refrain from a trip up this landmark. Even those in good physical condition may find themselves huffing and puffing on the way up.

A visit begins with a 10-minute film about the history of the lighthouse, which was built in 1873 in response to the shipwreck of the *Lady Elgin*. Nearly 300 people drowned off the Evanston shore. It's not surprising then that in 1908 Charles William Pearson penned a poem that described Grosse Point as "A dreaded point when the north winds roar." Because of its role in maritime commerce between the late 1800s and early 1900s, the lighthouse was named a National Historic Monument in 1999, one of only seven landmark lights in the country. A museum in the keeper's house shows a few historic objects, and a garden is planted with flowers that attract butterflies. But the real attraction here is the lighthouse itself.

KID-FRIENDLY EATS Bring a blanket and a picnic lunch, and eat in the park just north of the Evanston Art Center, which is next to the lighthouse. A concession truck sometimes visits when the beach behind the art center is open. The simple **Noyes Street Cafe** (828 Noyes St., tel. 847/475–8683) serves some American food as well as Greek specialties. For other options, *see* the Mitchell Museum of the American Indian.

2601 Sheridan Rd., Evanston

 $4 ages 13 and up,
$2 children 6–12

 Tours June–Sept, Sa–Su 2, 3, and 4

847/328-6961

 6 and up

Pass through a small room with items the keepers used, and begin the climb. The winding cast-iron-grate staircase has steep steps, which get smaller nearer the top. Little windows along the way reveal views of the lake and the adjoining neighborhood, but the best view comes when you crawl into the cramped space with the light or step out onto a narrow walkway. To the east is vast Lake Michigan, to the south the Chicago skyline, and to the north the tree-lined, curving shore of suburban communities.

Legend has it that though the French lens was destined for a southern lighthouse, it was buried in sand during the Civil War and rerouted to Evanston afterward. The first light was provided by an oil lamp, but an electric light was installed in 1922. In fact, the lighthouse is still a beacon for small boats, not to mention adventuresome climbers.

HEY, KIDS! At night you can see the light in action not only from the lake, but also from the west. It flashes 1½ seconds on, 2 seconds off, 1½ seconds on, and 10 seconds off. Try timing it.

KEEP IN MIND To grade-schoolers, it can seem like a long way up those steep curving stairs. Be ready for some awkward hand holding (you must travel single file) and words of encouragement, if necessary. A few small landings make passing a little easier, but since only 12 people are allowed on the tour at a time, traffic jams don't generally occur. Ask your child to count all 141 steps; it can provide just enough of a distraction to keep complaints to a minimum.

THE GROVE

Pioneer Robert Kennicott, known as Illinois's first naturalist, spent his short 30-year life here from 1836 to 1866 and studied the plants and animals that lived alongside him. Today his house and the land around it are a National Historic Landmark. Tours of the home and of a one-room schoolhouse on the property are conducted by guides dressed in 19th-century clothing. In an 1860s log cabin, other costumed guides demonstrate the housework of yesteryear: sweeping dirt floors "clean" and scrubbing clothes on a washboard.

But like Kennicott himself, your children will probably be happiest making discoveries about the natural world. A wooden walkway meanders across a pond created by a glacier long, long ago. It's a good place to see floating plants, such as water lilies, and maybe a few turtles and toads, a salamander or two, dragonflies and damselflies, and whirligig beetles that spin on top of the water. In the woods are cottonwood trees, whose roots drink water from the pond, as well as black willows, some 90 feet tall, whose bark and twigs were used by Native Americans to cure headaches.

KEEP IN MIND Just like their less-pesky animal cousins, mosquitoes like it here. Come with clothes that cover you and, if you must, insect repellent for the wooded trails. Interestingly, you won't find mosquitoes near the buildings. The woods also contain poison ivy, so don't leave the paths.

HEY, KIDS! Once you've developed an eagle eye for spotting birds and other animals in the wild, see if you can find an owl named Mrs. Hoot, who lives in a large cage outdoors. This great horned owl has feathers in various shades of gray, so she blends into her environment very well. And since she's nocturnal—that is, she spends her days sleeping—she'll be very still while you're visiting.

1421 Milwaukee Ave., Glenview

847/299-6096

 Free; Pioneer Skills Workshops $15 ages 15 and up, $10 children 5–14

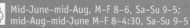 Mid-June–mid-Aug, M–F 8–6, Sa–Su 9–5; mid-Aug–mid-June M–F 8–4:30, Sa–Su 9–5

4 and up

Children can look closer at some of the wetland's creatures at the large interpretive center, near a Native American teepee. Turtles of all sizes move slowly from rock to rock and pull themselves into their shells for a rest in a large aquarium. There are also fish and snakes and a white ferret named Flour. On weekends naturalists offer extra activities, focusing on life in the pond or amphibians or bird migration. The center's children's programs include Pioneer Skills Workshops, about once a month, featuring candle-making, weaving, butter churning, and cooking up pioneer stew, as well as free, hands-on activities and encounters with native domestic animals. Annual events, for which there is a small charge, include Grove Heritage Days, with living-history demonstrations, storytelling, and a barn dance, as well as a Folk Fest. But even without a special event, the Grove is a wonderful place to visit for a little living history and a lot of living things.

KID-FRIENDLY EATS Previously allowed, picnics are now discouraged at the Grove, and no food or drink is sold except during special events. A few family-friendly restaurants are located nearby, including **Dappers** (4520 W. Lake Ave., tel. 847/699–0020), **T.G.I. Friday's** (4513 W. Lake Ave., tel. 847/298–9966), and **Wendy's** (4610 W. Lake Ave., tel. 847/824–1879).

HANCOCK OBSERVATORY

Carl Sandburg called Chicago the "Stormy, husky, brawling, City of the Big Shoulders" long before today's skyscrapers muscled their way into the skyline. Fitting right in among its broad-shouldered brethren is the John Hancock Center, dubbed Big John. The tallest building in the world when it was finished in 1970, it is now Chicago's third-tallest, "dwarfed" by the Sears Tower (*see below*) and the Amoco Building. Needless to say there's quite a view from the observatory on the 94th floor.

The trip to the top begins at the lower level, in an area that has been arranged to look like a construction site. A video details the construction of the building, which took four years to complete. Then comes the speedy elevator ride; it takes a little more than 40 seconds and might make your ears pop.

The observatory has a lot to look at within it, but it's the spectacular view outside that will catch your eye first. Walk all the way around to gaze in every direction. To the east are Lake

HEY, KIDS! Have your picture taken on the window-washers' scaffolding set up inside the observatory. Pose while climbing a girder like those used to construct the building. Both are in front of a large photo of buildings far below, so your snapshot will seem realistic. Or make an e-postcard ($2). A machine equipped with a digital camera not only takes your picture against a Chicago backdrop, but also lets you record a message. Your personalized postcard will then be sent via e-mail.

Michigan and Navy Pier. To the north you can see Oak Street Beach and, on a clear day, even Wisconsin. To the west stretch the United Center (home of the Bulls), O'Hare Airport, expressways, and suburbs as far as the eye can see, and to the south the skyscrapers stand tall. If your children want a close-up view, they can opt for virtual or reality. An interactive computer video lets you zoom in on spots around the city, and talking telescopes let you see things up close while listening to the sounds of the city and commentary in a choice of English, French, Japanese, or Spanish. When you've seen enough of today's Chicago, check out the wall of historical photographs that depicts how the city grew. The brave of heart can even walk outside (don't worry, it's heavily screened, and there's a sturdy railing) to check out the atmosphere at 1,000 feet above street level.

KEEP IN MIND

There may be a wait—as long as ½ hour at times—to take the elevator up to the observatory and also a wait to take it down, so plan accordingly. Saturdays are the busiest, Sundays are not so busy, and evenings are also good, especially if you want to see the city in lights. Once you get to the top, you can stay as long as you like.

KID-FRIENDLY EATS

The **Cheesecake Factory** (875 N. Michigan Ave., tel. 312/337–1101) serves over 30 kinds of cheesecake. Courtyard seating and live music are sometimes offered. Sandwiches at **Chicago Flat Sammies** (811 N. Michigan Ave., tel. 312/664–BRED), in the Pumping Station, are made with bread dough that's flattened before baking. **Foodlife** (835 N. Michigan Ave., Water Tower Place mezzanine level, tel. 312/335–3663) serves wraps, Asian noodles, and sandwiches. The market next door sells takeout.

HAROLD WASHINGTON PLAY-LOT PARK

Harold Washington, Chicago's first African-American mayor, passed away while still in office in 1987. What better tribute to a man interested in the well-being of children than a playground, and this one is something special. At the entrance is a sculpture of an open book with a relief portrait and quote of Washington's: "I see a Chicago of educational excellence and equality in which all children can learn to function in this ever-more complex society." Since children learn about the world through play, this is the perfect place to continue their education.

The park's centerpiece is a big wooden red, white, and black ship that seems to be waiting for children to climb aboard and take imaginary journeys. It "floats" on a soft blue rubberized surface that doesn't hurt the occasional "kid overboard." A wooden castle encourages another whole set of make-believe games. Metal equipment in cheerful primary colors is divided into two areas. One has spring-based dinosaur riders, baby swings, ladders, and bridges that are all just the right size for younger children. The other is designed to challenge the

HEY, KIDS!

If you're a triker, ride your three-wheeler on a path just for you (no bikes allowed). Running all around the playlot, the path is also made for wheelchairs, and spray pools and the ship are accessible, too. Don't worry: You can always see your parents.

KEEP IN MIND Packing for the playground has never been so complicated. If the weather is nice and hot, remember to bring towels to dry your children off after a spray pool session. A swimsuit is a good idea, too. Kids can change in the rest rooms. If the weather is even a little cool, bring an extra layer of warm clothes. Since the park is right across from the lake, it can be colder here than where you came from. The park has drinking fountains and an occasional ice-cream truck but no place to buy other food, so come prepared.

Hyde Park Blvd. from 51st to 53rd Sts.

 Free

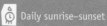 Daily sunrise–sunset

312/747-6620

 2–12

physical prowess of older kids, who clamber over monkey bars, tire swings, tunnels, rings, ladders, and slides, including one that's wide enough for two. A sandbox with sloped edges might actually get toddlers to sit for a while, and two spray pools with soft surfaces keep both big and little ones cool when the weather gets hot. In one, water sprays into the air as well as out of the mouths of sea horses.

There are plenty of benches for parents to sit, relax, and supervise, and since the playlot is surrounded by a low-level wrought-iron fence with only one exit, children aren't likely to escape without you. The two-block-long park around the playlot is grass-covered and has plenty of tall, shady trees and enough open space to play Frisbee.

KID-FRIENDLY EATS The park is the perfect place for a picnic, thanks to green grass all around and a lakefront setting with a splendid view of the city in the background. The **Dixie Kitchen and Bake Shop** (5225 S. Harper Ave., tel. 773/363–4943) has Cajun food and grilled-cheese sandwiches, hamburgers, and chicken nuggets. Familiar fare can be found at **McDonald's** (1344 E. 53rd St., tel. 773/493–1622) and **Boston Market** (1424 E. 53rd St., tel. 773/288–2600).

HEALTH WORLD

Kids may think that health and fun don't go together, but the more than 200 hands-on activities in this three-level museum will prove them wrong. Here children can discover how to keep themselves and the planet healthy while indeed having a good time.

Even big kids are bowled over by Kelly, nicknamed the Big Kid, who seems to be bowled over, too. An 85-foot-long fiberglass girl in a Little League uniform is stretched out on the floor near the entrance. Even reclining on her back she is two stories tall. Kids can walk inside and discover the details of human anatomy, crawling through her heart if they wish. In her backpack, also known as the Brain Theater, they can see a multimedia presentation, showing how a child's body reacts on a typical day. For example, when Kelly falls off her bike, they'll see what happens in her ear when she loses her balance.

Your children can visit the grocery store area and learn what good foods to choose. They can watch a puppet show about how germs invade daily life and then get a firsthand look

HEY, KIDS! Near Kelly, some gadgets—even good for 3-year-olds—let you test your strength and coordination. Squeeze a lever and watch a numbered scale light up, measuring your strength. See how long you can hang from a horizontal bar and how high you can jump. Listen for the sound that reveals how high you leaped. The higher the jump, the higher the pitch. There are enough gadgets to go around, so you won't have to wait too long for a turn.

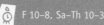

at the concept by washing their hands with Glow Germ lotion and looking at them under ultraviolet light to see if they've gotten rid of all the germs. The results might lead to more energetic hand washing in the future.

Kids can discover potential dangers in your house, practice what to do to escape a fire, and even dial 911 and hear a message like the real thing. They can try out their knowledge of bike safety by pedaling through a virtual village and experience what it feels like riding uphill and downhill with the wind blowing. They can also pretend to be a doctor, dressing in scrubs and performing pretend surgery or using instruments to diagnose problems. There is a place to test hearing, to find out what doctors see when they examine ears, and to fill a cavity in an oversize tooth. To find out about the health of the environment, your children can climb into Pete's Treehouse and Joey's Ranger Station. A visit to the museum is not only enlightening; it's good, clean, healthy fun.

KID-FRIENDLY EATS The museum's **Georgi's Garden Cafe** has child-friendly food, including turkey sandwiches, Italian beef sandwiches, pizza, and chicken tenders. The dessert menu offers fresh-baked cookies and, as befits the museum's mission, such healthy choices as fruit cups and apple-sauce.

KEEP IN MIND If you and your child are ready for it, head to the area that gently explains where babies come from. You'll want to stay close at hand to guide your child through and be prepared for discussions afterward.

INDIAN BOUNDARY PARK

Sometimes a neighborhood park is more than *just* a neighborhood park. At this one, there's a little something extra. The playground contains a vast wooden structure with all sorts of places to swing and slide, climb and hide. There's even a log locomotive for make-believe fast getaways. A spray pool is the ideal place to pass hot summer days (mid-June through Labor Day). It's like running through the jet from an opened fire hydrant, only legal.

The park also has its own miniature zoo, which started in the 1920s when someone donated a bear. Recently it was almost shut down, but a community outcry kept it open. Managed by the Lincoln Park Zoo, the zoolet has several white-tailed deer; some domestic goats, raised for their milk; several pigmy goats from Africa; an alpaca; and two mute swans. Incidentally, in 12th-century England, mute swans were considered so extraordinary that only members of royalty were allowed to own them. Your children mustn't try to feed the animals. They have their own specific diets to keep them healthy and must be hungry enough at closing time to want the treats they're given to lure them inside.

HEY, KIDS!

The alpaca you'll see in the zoo is from a family of South American mammals that includes the llama. However, though the llama is used primarily as a pack animal, the alpaca is raised for its wool. Unfortunately, you're not allowed to touch the alpaca to find out what that wool feels like.

KEEP IN MIND If it's a warm day, remember to bring swimsuits and towels so your kids will be able to play in the spray pool and dry off afterwards. Lamentably, there's no parking lot, so you'll have to search for a spot on the street and walk. If you want more activity than a stroll to the car, you can walk to nearby Warren Park, which has an outdoor track designed for in-line skating that becomes a skating rink in the winter.

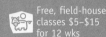 2500 W. Lunt Ave.

 312/742-7887

Free, field-house classes $5–$15 for 12 wks

Daily 6 AM–11 PM. Field house M–F 9–9, Sa–Su 9–5. Zoo daily 9–4:30. Concerts July–Aug, some Su 5

All ages

Next to the zoo, an exhibit area has houses to attract birds and bats and vegetation to attract butterflies. A lagoon with a geyser shooting up in the middle brings wild ducks and Canada geese. Please don't feed these animals either; it would attract more and more birds, and the lagoon would become overpopulated. The park also has many grassy areas and trees, so though there is no place to play baseball or basketball, there is room to throw a Frisbee. Surprisingly, a field house is the venue for the arts rather than sports. Classes in art, dance, and drama are offered here throughout the year.

In summer, you can stay for a free Sunday evening concert, featuring musical fare from salsa to the blues to classical. It's a fitting end to a full, rich day in the park.

KID-FRIENDLY EATS Pack your own picnic. You won't be alone. Neighborhood residents bring food that reflects their many different ethnic backgrounds and often eat it while listening to the music of their particular culture. Barbecuing, once permitted, is no longer allowed. For dessert, you can count on ice-cream trucks coming regularly throughout the day.

INTERNATIONAL MUSEUM OF
SURGICAL SCIENCE

The faint of heart or stomach may want to skip this museum, but others will be fascinated by its large collection of historical objects designed for healing, many more imaginative than effective. The museum is housed in a 1917 mansion inspired by a French château on the property of Versailles, but while the building is elegant, its four floors of exhibits tend to the creepy. And except for one button in the drugstore, which you can push to hear about a pharmacist's profession around 1900, the museum is a traditional one where you look but don't touch.

Among the exhibits are bright-colored handmade objects the Aztecs used to rid people of various ills and 4,000-year-old skulls from Peru with holes bored into them so that evil spirits could escape. Skull boring was also used more recently to cure blindness and insanity. (A skeleton in a classroom setting shows how surgeons finally learned about human anatomy—thank goodness.) A case with objects from the Civil War shows some bullets and an amputation kit, and a mural—one of many throughout the museum depicting surgery—graphically

HEY, KIDS! Play the first-floor Germ Find game and learn a bit about germs—like how doctors didn't know about them before 1850. Look at a photo of a pre–germ theory operation. Would you want to be operated on by surgeons without gloves or masks, while paying spectators watch, the way they once did?

shows a man writhing in pain while his leg is being amputated. An old-fashioned drugstore has jars and bottles and boxes of various concoctions on the shelves. As preposterous as it sounds, there are even special cigarettes that were supposed to help people with bronchitis. A re-created turn-of-the-20th-century physician's office contains tools ready and waiting to deliver babies, remove abscesses or lumps, or even bleed a patient suffering from a cold or insomnia. There is also a room with early X-ray equipment as well as a 1950s Buster Brown Shoe Fitter, which unbelievably used X-rays to check the fit of new shoes. It was around this time that scientists began to realize that doses of radiation could be harmful.

Don't be surprised if your children come away wondering how sick people ever survived all these treatments, let alone the illnesses, and thankful to live today rather than in olden times.

KID-FRIENDLY EATS The **Big Bowl** (6 E. Cedar St., tel. 312/640–8888) is an Asian noodle shop. The children's menu includes Chinese crunchy chicken sticks, satay, potstickers, barbecued chicken, and plain egg noodles, and the menu illustrates how to use chopsticks. The **Corner Bakery** (1121 N. State St., tel. 312/787–1969) makes fresh salads, sandwiches, pastas, and pizzas.

KEEP IN MIND Although the exhibits don't offer any hands-on activities, if you can get together a group of five people and reserve ahead of time, you can watch a video called "The Brutal Craft," which traces the history of amputation, first practiced by handymen because they had the necessary tools. Then you can re-enact a Civil War amputation, with kids playing the parts of the doctor, the patient, and the two people who had to hold the patient down during the operation. They haven't lost a patient yet.

JOHN G. SHEDD AQUARIUM

More than 70% of the earth is covered with water, remaining largely hidden from us. But not at this dual facility. The aquarium, housed in a Greek-style building, opened in 1930 and contains more than 100 exhibits of fish from the world's oceans, rivers, and lakes. The attached white-marble indoor oceanarium, whose curved wall of windows overlooks Lake Michigan, opened in 1991 as a home for marine mammals.

At the oceanarium, your family can watch Pacific white-sided dolphins. Five times a day their caretakers let them show off the natural behaviors they've developed to adapt to their environment: leaping in the air, walking on their tails, and breaching (jumping and slapping their bodies against the water). Stroll through re-created habitats reflecting the Pacific coastline from Northern California to Alaska's Prince William Sound. Follow a "nature trail" to seals and sea otters. They're great fun to watch, as are the penguins (an exception to the mammals-only policy). The Underwater Viewing Gallery yields an unusual view of these animals. Hands-on activities teach all about marine mammals.

HEY, KIDS! The aquarium and oceanarium are home to several animals and ecosystems that are endangered: the Tahitian land snail; the South American bonytongue (a fish that people along the Amazon River eat); the African cichlid; the sea otter; various sea turtles; the Cayman Island rock iguana (that lizard with spines on its back); and coral reefs, which are threatened by global warming, human collectors, ship anchors, and runoff from land. See if you can find them all.

1200 S. Lake Shore Dr.

 T–Su $11 ages 12 and up, $9 children 3–11; M $6 ages 12 and up, $5 children. Aquarium only $5–$6 less

Late May–Labor Day, daily 9–6; early Sept–late May, M–F 9–5, Sa–Su 9–6

 312/939–2438

All ages

The aquarium has weird and wonderful fish in darkened galleries, so you feel like you're underwater, too. The most popular place is the Caribbean Reef at feeding time. A diver wearing a microphone goes into the 90,000-gallon tank and describes the creatures and their diet. Don't worry: The big ones won't eat the little ones. A tank within a tank separates them. Try to find green moray eels (up to 6 feet long) or nurse sharks, both excellent hiders. You can't miss the barracuda, though, with its long pointed jaw and torpedo-shape body. Amazon Rising: Seasons of the River takes you on a boardwalk through a rain forest. You'll see life when the river is low and then, after passing a wall of rain (no, you won't get wet), see it transformed after the flooding season. Watch for sloths, anacondas, piranhas, stingrays, and other eye-openers.

KID-FRIENDLY EATS The aquarium has a cafeteria-style restaurant called the **Bubble Net** (tel. 312/692–3277), which looks over Lake Michigan. It offers Pizza Hut pizza, hamburgers, hot dogs, chicken fingers, sandwiches, and salads. **Soundings** (tel. 312/692–3277), a sit-down restaurant that also has lake views, serves more sophisticated food for adults as well as children's fare: a peanut butter and jelly sandwich served with fruit, spaghetti, or chicken fingers and fries.

KOHL CHILDREN'S MUSEUM

Though this two-story museum is enjoyed by infants through young grade-schoolers, even adults rediscover their inner child at this quintessential kindergarten. It's a nurturing place where kids play to their heart's content without realizing they're learning.

Though you may find grocery shopping a chore, your children will probably love the museum's miniature supermarket. Choosing what to buy, weighing produce, and operating the checkout scanner, youngsters are definitely in control. After a hectic time shopping, they can take a break in the store's replica café, but nobody rests for long because there's too much to do. Next might be playing in the People exhibit, which celebrates our diversity. The hospital nursery has baby dolls in many colors, all waiting to be cuddled. Push a button to hear the universal sounds of an 18-minute-old newborn. A dollhouse has dolls representing different ethnic groups, who manage to play very well together. In the Construction Zone, your kids can don hard hats and put together a child-size house using bricks and tiles and then landscape it with soft-sculpture flowers. In the StarMax Technology Center, software helps with reading, math, or

HEY, KIDS! Check out the activity in the People exhibit that's called Beautiful People; it demonstrates that beautiful people come in all colors. When you dance to music in a darkened space here, your silhouette is projected larger than life on a big screen and constantly changes colors. Each one is as extraordinary as the one before, as are other people's silhouettes, also in ever-changing colors. Try to get your parents to try it, too. Groovy.

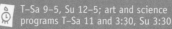

$5 ages 1 and up

art, along with being fun. The H2O exhibit is in its own room, where anything can get wet except the kids, who wear waterproof aprons. Balls are cranked up an incline, roll through tubes along the ceiling, and then fall back into a stream where children are playing. Children can dam the stream and channel it in various directions.

Some exhibits are permanent, but new ones come along, too. Art and science programs offer hands-on activities ranging from celebrating Elvis Presley's birthday to making sundials to painting with sponges. The museum's motto is "I hear and I forget, I see and I remember, I touch and I understand." Everywhere here, you see little hands busy touching and understanding.

KEEP IN MIND

There are places here for kids to play on their own and others where you can and should play with them. It's best to follow your kids' lead and also watch what other people are doing. By both interacting and observing, you can enjoy your children's discoveries all the more—and so can they.

KID-FRIENDLY EATS Everybody loves **Walker Bros. Original Pancake House** (153 Green Bay Rd., tel. 847/251–6000), especially Sunday morning (it's crowded). Kids love the silver-dollar pancakes: chocolate chip, blueberry, or plain. At **Panera Bread** (1199 Wilmette Ave., tel. 847/853–8170) children can get sandwiches, soup, and chocolate-chip cookies or muffins. Take home a loaf of bread. **Homer's Restaurant & Ice Cream Parlor** (1237 Green Bay Rd., tel. 847/251–0477) serves meals, but the star is the ice cream.

THE L

A lot of cities have subways, but Chicago has an elevated train known as the L. A trip around the Loop—originally named for the cable cars that circled this business and shopping district and still encircled by the 1897 L tracks—and out into a residential neighborhood is a great way to see the city. The trains screech and groan, but they keep on traveling, giving you a close-up, second-story view in some parts and a ground-level or underground peek in others.

The L has several different lines. A good excursion follows the Brown Line from the Merchandise Mart out of the city center to the terminal at Kimball. Crossing the Chicago River, your children can see the city's bridges and boats traveling to and from Lake Michigan. At Wells and Lake streets, the L meets up with lines going in various directions. This was the world's busiest intersection in the 1930s, when a train came through every 20 seconds. As the train continues, urge your kids to look for signs of preservation and growth: scaffolding on old buildings being renovated and heavy equipment where new ones are being built. Buildings built in 1871, right after

HEY, KIDS!

Ask a parent to point out the corner of State and Lake streets, where a humorous parking garage designed by architect Stanley Tigerman sits. The awning looks like car tires, and the facade resembles a Rolls-Royce's grille. Its turquoise color was used on 1957 Chevrolets.

KEEP IN MIND Don't lecture your kids on architectural history during the ride. Chances are they won't remember it, and the train won't stop long enough. The only date to mention is 1871, when fire destroyed Chicago, which was then rebuilt from the bottom up . . . and up and up. This trip is best seen as an opportunity for kids to observe the urban landscape, so they can gradually appreciate architecture and urban planning. For more, the Chicago Architecture Foundation (224 S. Michigan Ave., tel. 312/922–3432) has a book for families called *Look Up* and also gives Loop train tours.

The Loop; suggested entrance, Merchandise Mart, Wells St. south of Kinzie St.

 Brown Line M–F 5:15 AM–12 AM, Sa 6:15 AM–8:15 PM; different hrs for other lines

312/836–7000

 $1.50 ages 12 and up, 75¢ children 7–11

6 and up

the Great Chicago Fire, are easy to recognize, because they're only four or five stories high, the limit people would climb before the advent of passenger elevators. They also have tall, skinny windows.

As the train turns onto Van Buren Street, watch for the white terra-cotta Insurance Exchange Building, built between 1914 and 1928. One of its corners looks like it was cut off, but it was designed that way so the train wouldn't hit it.

The train continues through the city past many interesting structures and ways of life, finally recrossing the Chicago River, coming down to ground level, and skirting people's backyards. To return downtown, you can board another train at Kimball without paying a second fare, but you might want to change at Fullerton to the Red Line, which stops along State Street. The Red goes underground, making it seem like a theme park ride, only gentler.

KID-FRIENDLY EATS If you take the Red Line to return, you can get off at the Chicago Avenue and State Street stop (see the Hancock Observatory for places to eat). If you get off at Grand Avenue and State Street, you'll be near a lot of theme restaurants (see Chicago Duck Tours, Double Decker Bus Tours, and Ed Debevic's Short Order Deluxe).

LAKEFRONT BIKE WAY

Fitness and fun go together along this 18½-mile bicycle path that follows the beautiful shoreline of Lake Michigan. You can spend a pleasant day just riding along the lake with your family, perhaps pausing for a picnic, or you can stop at any of the many museums and other cultural and recreational attractions along the way.

The parks and beaches all along the bikeway have metered parking spots, so you can start at any point and explore the lakefront bit by bit. If you want to pedal the bike trail's southern end, park at Promontory Point (55th St. and the lake), where there is a beautiful view of the city and nearby Harold Washington Playlot Park (*see above*). From here you can ride toward the Museum of Science and Industry (*see below*) and the Japanese-style Osaka Garden in Jackson Park.

Another option is to park along Columbus Drive between Monroe and Jackson drives and then head east toward the lake to find the bike path. This gives you the option of riding

HEY, KIDS! Don't forget to wear your helmet. Experts say that to be really safe, it should be level on your head, not tilted either forward or back. If your helmet's on right, you should be able to look up and see its front edge.

Parallel to Lake Shore Dr., between Hollywood Ave. and 71st St.

 Free

 Daily sunrise–11 PM

 312/747-2474 Chicago Park District

8 and up

south or north. If you go south, you'll pass by all the boats in Monroe Harbor, to the east of Grant Park, and on to the park's Buckingham Fountain (Lake Shore Dr. south of Jackson Dr.), which was built in 1927 and inspired by a fountain at Versailles. Farther south is the city's triumvirate of museums—the Adler Planetarium and Astronomy Museum, the Field Museum of Natural History, and the John G. Shedd Aquarium (*see above*)—surrounded by the park area known as the Museum Campus. If you go north from Grant Park, you'll pass by Oak Street Beach, one of Chicago's most popular, and on to the Lincoln Park Zoo. You'll pass a replica of a Haidan Indian totem pole and Montrose Harbor, all the while watching people having picnics; playing baseball, soccer, and basketball; flying kites; and, like you, having a good time.

KID-FRIENDLY EATS There are concession stands and cafés all along the bikeway. Two good places to stop are the Lincoln Park Zoo (*see below*) and Buckingham Fountain. Of course, there are also plenty of places to picnic.

KEEP IN MIND Call the Chicago Park District to get a map of the bikeway. The path can be crowded with cyclists, in-line skaters, joggers, and walkers, so make sure that your children know the rules of the road: Stay to the right, between the center yellow line and the white warning lines on the edge, and allow faster modes of transport to pass. Watch for "zebra stripes," which warn of upcoming intersections, and three yellow stripes at the entrance to a path, which mean bikes aren't allowed. If you need to stop, move off the bikeway.

LATTOF YMCA

E veryone in the family can have fun at the Lattof YMCA. It has the usual activities you'd expect at a Y—cardiovascular- and weight-training areas, an indoor running track, nine handball/racquetball courts, an aerobics room, and three indoor pools—but there's also a lot more, all available with a guest pass.

A triple-decker play area called 'Mazing Kids makes children happy while they're working on their large-motor skills. They can crawl through tubes, climb on nets and webs, try out mini-slides, or jump around joyously in a pit of bright-color balls. Children under 5 need adult supervision, but that can be fun, too, since you can join them.

Older children can romp on their own or take part in Generation X–type sports while you engage in other activities in the facility. While you work out on exercise bicycles, they can work on their gravity-defying tricks at the skate park, as long as you sign a waiver and the weather permits. Possessing just the right surface for skateboarding, the park has a half-pipe, rails,

KID-FRIENDLY EATS Lattof has a variety of vending machines dispensing sandwiches, soup, chips, beverages, and candy, which can then be eaten at tables in the pool area. You can also bring your own food. Plans are under way to open a café in the building.

300 E. Northwest Hwy.,
Des Plaines

847/296-3376

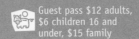 Guest pass $12 adults,
$6 children 16 and
under, $15 family

 M-F 5:15 AM-10 PM, Sa-Su 6-6 (closed Su Memorial
Day-Labor Day).

 2 and up

and everything else needed to master the techniques of this sport. You may not want to watch, but you'll be happy to know that helmets and wrist guards are required and that knee and elbow pads are highly recommended. Lattof also offers in-line skating and skateboard lessons.

Also in the extreme vein, the Y offers courses in climbing; upon completion, your children can use the 25-foot climbing wall. For a different kind of climbing, your young adventurers can make their way through a constructed indoor cave with hand- and footholds or tackle a high-ropes course. Its 17 elements include the Burma Bridge, the Kitten Crawl, Earthquake Tremor, and the Floating Bridge, all suspended in air. Classes, which teach the intricacies of various techniques, are a must. All in all, your young daredevils can get their fill of extreme sports, while you can try hard not to worry. After a day of X games at the Y, you'll all be ready for some Z's.

KEEP IN MIND Remember that no two children are alike. Some will love the physical challenges in store here, while others may be fearful. A little coaxing can do the trick, but in some cases, pushing a child who isn't ready is counterproductive. The goal should be to have fun, and increased self-confidence is often the by-product.

LET'S DRESS UP

Parents are always telling their kids they can be anything they want to be when they grow up. But why wait? At Let's Dress Up, your children can try on their dreams now. All they need is a fertile imagination and the right clothes. And the choice of clothes here—elaborate kid-size costumes with realistic details—is plenty large.

Kids can choose between total fantasy and quasi-reality, between good guys and bad guys. Although boys tend to be the ones to transform themselves into knights, dragons, and cowboys, while girls gravitate to fairy-tale princesses and the like, both genders can suit up in whatever suits their fancies. Children can take their inspiration from *Star Wars,* dressing as C3PO or Darth Vader, or from MTV, wearing outfits made from as much glitter as spandex. Girls (or boys with a good sense of style and/or humor) might opt for a bridal gown with a bouffant skirt, layers of lace, and a cathedral train or one with elegant satin and a beaded bodice. From the ridiculous to the sublime and back again they all go, putting together perfectly coordinated outfits or mixing and matching as the mood strikes.

KID-FRIENDLY EATS There are plenty of familiar if uninspiring fast-food chains in Lombard: **Boston Market** (150 E. Roosevelt Rd., tel. 630/620–0400), **Burger King** (401 E. Roosevelt Rd., tel. 630/916–9499), **McDonald's** (300 E. Roosevelt Rd., tel. 630/620–4280), and **Wendy's** (820 E. Roosevelt Rd., tel. 630/495–2730). At **Edwardo's** (904 Army Trail Rd., Carol Stream, tel. 630/830–9600), part of a chain, children can get mostaccioli or a 6-inch pizza with one topping.

1222 S. Highland Ave., Lombard;
960 Army Trail Rd., Carol Stream

$6 1 hr, $8 1½ hrs children 13
and under; tea party $1.25

Lombard M–Sa 11–6, Su 12–6;
Carol Stream daily 12–6

630/932–7529 Lombard,
630/830–5800 Carol Stream

3–13

Make-believe doesn't stop with the right wardrobe. Rooms are decorated as matching settings, such as a ballroom fit for princes and princesses. In this department, the Carol Stream location is bigger and better, especially in its "boy" offerings. Carol Stream has a gingerbread cottage, gazebo, general store, and Planet Wonder, which includes a medieval castle, campground, and a western setting with a saloon, a jail, and an outhouse. There is also a dimly lit Space Room, where pretend astronauts will feel out of this world.

HEY, KIDS! Ask your parents if you can stay for a tea party, which takes place every hour. You can keep your costume on while you drink lemonade and eat cookies, pretzels, or another tasty snack.

KEEP IN MIND Let's Dress Up has similar costumes for adults, too, so feel free to join in the fun. But try to let your children call the shots; remember this is make-believe. Because there are no dressing rooms, your kids should come wearing clothes that aren't too bulky—such as shorts and a T-shirt or a leotard—so that the costumes will fit nicely over them.

LIFELINE THEATRE KIDSERIES

Lifeline Theatre is an award-winning professional theater company known for its creative stage adaptations of such literary works as *Pride and Prejudice.* What this ensemble of 17 adapters, composers, actors, directors, designers, and visual artists does for grown-ups, they also do for children.

KidSeries plays are original adaptations of favorite children's books and often include charming music written especially for them. The same high standards and originality apply equally to these productions, which are presented in the company's cozy 100-seat theater. Though the plays for young people are thoroughly professional, they have a feeling of innocence and spontaneity, whimsy and quirkiness—almost as if they were put on by children in their own backyard.

Take, for example, a recent production of Virginia Lee Burton's *Mike Mulligan and His Steam Shovel,* which included some lively country-and-western songs. Some theater companies

HEY, KIDS!

Head to the lobby and its comfy oversize chair from a production of *Bunnicula.* You'll have to climb up into it or get a boost, and only two people are allowed in it at a time. Why don't you share your turn with your sibling or parent?

KEEP IN MIND
The neighborhood looks a bit run-down, but never fear. Families have been coming to this theater safely and happily coming back for years. Nevertheless, you wouldn't want to linger long or roam the streets, where sidewalks are littered and loitering is common. You shouldn't have any problem finding metered parking on Morse Avenue. Theater patrons also can find free parking three blocks directly north of the theater at the corner of Glenwood and Estes avenues in the Trilogy, Inc. lot.

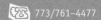

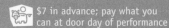

might have portrayed Mary Anne the steam shovel as a clanking contraption, but the Lifeline artistic team simply dressed her in overalls and a hard hat. In fact, costumes and decor are often kept simple yet are still very imaginative. However, an adaptation of Daniel Pinkwater's *Lizard Music* saw reptiles with very elaborate headpieces sing an inventive recitative score. Hardly your everyday lizard music! A puppet also played an important role in the story, as puppets do in many productions.

After each performance, actors come out to the lobby to meet kids, give autographs, and answer questions. So it should come as no surprise that the theater has a faithful following, many of whom expressed their spirit by coming to a presentation of *101 Dalmatians* bedecked in black spots on a white background. But no matter what the play, your children will undoubtedly enjoy its imaginativeness, humor, and warmheartedness and come away feeling that all is right with the world.

KID-FRIENDLY EATS Some people think that the **Heartland Cafe** (7000 N. Glenwood Ave., tel. 773/465–8005), which opened in the mid-'70s and has kept that era's ambience, is a vegetarian restaurant, but this popular place also serves chicken and fish. So the kids' menu includes not only peanut butter and jelly, tofu hot dogs, and macaroni and cheese, but also chicken fingers. **Leona's** (6935 N. Sheridan Rd., tel. 773/764–5757) is part of a family-run chain that offers pizza and traditional Italian fare.

LINCOLN PARK ZOO

L ike many other zoos, this one showcases animals in settings resembling their natural habitats. What sets it apart are its manageable size and its free admission, both of which make it easy to see what you want and leave before anyone gets exhausted.

Pick up a free visitor guide from the Information Center at the east entrance, and decide what to see first. If your kids like big cats, they can see not only the African lion, a.k.a. the king of the jungle, but also the jaguar; the rare snow leopard; cheetahs, the fastest animals on land; and servals, who (in the wild) jump to catch birds. Among the primates, a howler monkey, whose call can be heard miles away, and some acrobatic white-cheeked gibbons swing from branch to branch in a rain-forest environment. Gorillas, chimpanzees, and orangutans are in the Great Ape House. The Small Mammal–Reptile House contains environments from four continents. You'll have to look closely to find snakes, sloths, and spiders hidden in the vegetation. Discovery Stations let your children get to know the animals better by touching related objects, such as a tortoise shell or porcupine quills.

KEEP IN MIND When your kids' (or your) energy level gets low, stop in at the Children's Zoo. Here kids of all ages can see newborn animals, and children over 5 can even touch some creatures, such as snakes (nonpoisonous ones, of course), a tortoise, rabbits, and guinea pigs. In the outdoor garden they can see an alpaca or watch an otter being fed fish and meat. In the Conservation Station they can touch such objects as hides, feathers, and bones.

Large mammals from Africa, including elephants and giraffes, show off their gigantic size in their own section. In the bear area, your children can see polar bears swimming and cute spectacled bears, who look like they're wearing glasses. For other swimmers, take the underground passageway at the Sea Lion Pool to see sea lions and seals underwater. The bird house contains exotic birds, though penguins and seabirds live elsewhere.

The Farm-in-the-Zoo could merit its own trip. Here children see firsthand where tomorrow's food comes from—piglets, chicks, and dairy cows. Annual events include Run for the Zoo and ZooFest (June), Spooky Zoo Spectacular (Halloween), and ZooLights Festival and Caroling to the Animals (Christmas). It's a lot to absorb—over 1,000 animals in all—in a small space.

TRANSPORTATION Free parking is theoretically available but can be hard to find, so you might opt for the paid parking on Cannon Drive. Public transportation is another solution. The No. 151 Sheridan Road bus stops at the zoo. On weekends between 9 and 7, a free trolley runs around the periphery of the zoo and to and from the Fullerton and Sedgewick L stops.

KID-FRIENDLY EATS Food carts sell hot dogs and ice cream. **Cafe Brauer,** in a historic Prairie-style building overlooking a pond, serves standard fare. Kids munch animal-shape fries (and other food-court options) in animal-shape chairs in the **Park Place Cafe.** The rooftop **Big Cats Cafe,** overlooking the birds of prey, lions, and Lake Michigan, offers sandwiches on various breads. Some people eat at **R.J. Grunts** (2056 Lincoln Park W, tel. 312/929–5363) for nostalgia's sake. (It had one of the first salad bars.) Others go for the burgers.

MEXICAN FINE ARTS CENTER MUSEUM

There are no borders at this museum. Everyone is welcome to celebrate Mexican culture, both traditional and contemporary, created in Mexico and in the United States. Several eclectic exhibits grace the museum each year: important archaeological finds; paintings whose images were used for Mexican calendars, such as depictions of mariachi musicians and Aztec legends; and works by the renowned photographer Graciela Iturbide as well as pieces from the museum's permanent collection, which contains folk art and works by such well-known artists as Orozco. Many of the museum's exhibits are accompanied by free Family Days, which include demonstrations, workshops, and even storytelling sessions for children.

Three times a year, the museum hosts free special events. A *Día de Muertos* (Day of the Dead) exhibition, from late September to early December, displays works of art inspired by this day, when the spirits of those who have died are allowed to return home. Altars like those made by Mexican families contain objects from the life of the deceased person, candles to represent the element of fire, incense to represent wind, and a special bread that stands

HEY, KIDS!

Don't be afraid of the special Day of the Dead skulls made of sugar. Mexican kids love them and exchange them with friends like valentines. As part of the event, a Mexican artist demonstrates skull decorating. And since they're made of sugar, they're edible. Yum!

KEEP IN MIND The museum is in the Pilsen neighborhood, which has a large Mexican population. Walking around the area and looking at the stores and restaurants immerses you even further in Mexican culture. To add to your sensory experience, pick up a map at the museum for a self-guided tour of local bakeries that make bread for the Day of the Dead festival. From mid-October to early November, store windows are painted with Day of the Dead imagery and the smell of sweet bread hangs in the air.

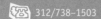 1852 W. 19th St.

 312/738–1503

Free

T–Su 10–5; Family Days
usually Su 2–4

4 and up

for the earth. Petals from a yellow flower are scattered along the path in front of houses to show spirits the way home.

An October–November event celebrates the life of Sor Juana, who lived in Mexico in the 17th century. Because women weren't given opportunities to excel, she entered a convent, where she was allowed to study. She became an accomplished writer, philosopher, and mathematician and has been called the first feminist of the Americas. Activities for children, such as an all-female mariachi-group performance—are usually part of the event. *Del Corazon,* which means "from the heart," takes place in April and May and includes performing arts events for all ages.

In September 2000 the museum will dedicate an outdoor plaza landscaped like ones in Mexico and will debut a new exhibition, including computer components for kids, that traces the history of Mexico from pre-Columbian times to the present.

KID-FRIENDLY EATS Mexican restaurants abound. **Nuevo León** (1515 W. 18th St., tel. 312/421–1517), painted outside with trellises and flowers, serves tacos, enchiladas, tamales, soups, and stews. **Polo's** (1454 W. 18th St., tel. 312/829–9377) is also worthwhile. Mexican bakeries make cookies and pastries in addition to Day of the Dead breads, and street vendors sell food ranging from warm corn on the cob with lime juice to mango slices.

MITCHELL MUSEUM OF THE
AMERICAN INDIAN

The Hollywood stereotypes that once defined Indians are gone, replaced at this museum, part of Kendall College, with a picture of a rich and diverse Native American culture and history. Your children will get a close-up view of native peoples and an understanding of how they used natural resources without exhausting them. Brick walls and red tile floors give an earthy, you-are-there feeling to the galleries, divided by geographical region.

The French explorers called the Great Lakes tribes the "People of the Rapids" because of their fearless canoeing. The exhibit shows a birch-bark canoe, snowshoes with caribou-hide webbing, and bags decorated with the glass beads that Europeans brought. A table full of "touchables" includes a leather ball that when tossed through a hoop attached to it improves hand-eye coordination—better than video games. Without a Home Depot, Native Americans made their tools, and your kids can try chipping away to sharpen a stone or wearing an anklet of deer toes to attract deer.

KEEP IN MIND Items in the touchable areas are labeled with names and descriptions, but not all the objects are self-explanatory. Ask a museum staff person to explain them.

2600 Central Park, Evanston

847/475–1030 or 847/866–1300

 $4 ages 13 and up

 T–F 10–6, Sa–Su 11–4

3 and up

Kachina dolls inhabit the Greater Southwest display. The Hopis believed the dolls embodied the spirits of nature and of their ancestors. Among the touchable objects here, the bull roarer is the most impressive. Swinging this piece of wood on a long string makes a truly frightening sound meant to scare wolves.

The tribes of the Plains are represented by elk-skin pants, a feather headdress, and an enormous bison hide. Kids can touch dried antelope hide and see how it was made into moccasins or an arrowhead bag. The Native Americans of the Northwest Coast are known for masks and totem poles. Both are represented: some monsterlike masks along with an authentic totem pole and totem-pole puzzle. Your children can try on a button blanket, decorated with 450 buttons and worn like a shawl.

KID-FRIENDLY EATS Try **Daruma** (2901 Central St., tel. 847/864–6633) for Japanese food, or buy sandwiches from **Foodstuffs** (2106 Central St., tel. 847/328–7704) and eat in the park. The **Bean Counter Cafe** (1932 Central St., tel. 847/332–1116) has kid sandwiches followed by pies with candy. **Prairie Joe's** (1921 Central St., tel. 847/491–0391) has kid fare and unusual ceiling decor.

HEY, KIDS! Try grinding dried corn kernels using a stone, as Native Americans did to make flat bread. It was one of the major occupations of women; in fact, they spent about two hours a day at it. Native Americans have been grinding corn ever since corn came from South America 1,500 to 2,000 years ago, and some traditionalists still do it today. It's a lot more work to make food this way than to microwave a bag of popcorn, don't you think?

MUSEUM OF BROADCAST
COMMUNICATIONS

Most kids don't realize that before there was color and cable, there was black and white and rabbit ears, and before that there was radio. Your children can return to those golden olden days, well before they (and you) were born, when families listened not just to music and news but also to dramas and comedy shows. And they listened together.

Start by taking a look at the old-fashioned radios, which look nothing like today's tiny, transistorized ones. Then check out the hands-on displays that make old radio shows accessible to kids. They can see the ventriloquist dummies Mortimer Snerd and Charlie McCarthy, Jack Benny's sidekicks, and can try to open the safe where the famous tightwad comedian stashed his cash. But beware. An alarm goes off if they succeed. If they open a particular closet door, they'll discover what happened when Fibber, in spite of all warnings, opened it every week on "Fibber McGee and Molly" and everything inside came tumbling out. On Saturday from 1 to 4, families can join the studio audience of a radio show called "Those Were the Days," on which the host introduces radio programs of the past.

HEY, KIDS!

Once you've seen Bozo, you might just want to clown around a little yourself. The museum store sells big red noses like the one the big goofy clown wore. Ask your parents if they had one when they were little, or even a Bozo punching bag.

KEEP IN MIND Your children might need help relating to the exhibits dealing with the history of radio and TV. If your knowledge doesn't go back further than dials and test patterns, you might want to bring along a grandparent or other older friend, who can share firsthand experiences of the early days of broadcasting.

Chicago Cultural Center, Michigan Ave. at Washington St.

312/629-6000

Free

M–Sa 10–4:30, Su 12–5

5 and up

TV has a place here, too. One exhibit showcases the puppets that performed on *Garfield Goose,* a popular children's show from the late '40s to the late '60s. Another lets you look at some award-winning commercials. Though they may not convince you to buy the product, they're good for a laugh.

Older children can become news anchors in a TV studio. For $20 each, including a video of the program to take home, your kids can don a sport jacket and read a script on a TelePrompTer in front of a camera. When the broadcast is over, the child's name will appear in the credits. (Call to make reservations for any day but Sunday.) For a $2 fee, you and your family can rent a booth and watch old TV programs from the museum's archives, such as *Ray Rayner; Kukla, Fran, and Ollie; Bozo's Circus;* and *Garfield Goose.* It can be worth it just to be able to all watch TV together.

KID-FRIENDLY EATS The building housing the museum has a **Corner Bakery** (*see* the Chicago Cultural Center). The **Big Downtown** (124 S. Wabash Ave., tel. 312/917–7399) has pizzas, sandwiches, hamburgers, and a dessert called the Big Shoulders brownie, named after Carl Sandburg's description of Chicago. Attention-getting city memorabilia enlivens the decor.

MUSEUM OF CONTEMPORARY ART

The exterior of this museum isn't very inviting, but once your children get a look at the artworks inside, dating from 1945 to the present, they're sure to think that contemporary art is cool. Some 100 works of the 3,500-piece permanent collection are usually on display. Kids are mesmerized by Alexander Calder's colorful sculptures, intrigued by bizarre surrealist works, and amazed to see vacuum cleaners turned into art. They'll be tempted to plop down on the giant fried-egg soft sculpture, but tell them not to.

Children also discover works where art and technology intersect. They can watch truisms file by on a neon sign and will probably get the giggles watching a video of a woman sucking her toe. A film of a woman's talking head projected onto a ball sticking out from under a mattress on the floor can be disturbing, but then contemporary art can be both humorous and unsettling. To learn more about it, kids can use touch-screen computers to assemble a work of art and play the role of a curator laying out an exhibit.

HEY, KIDS! Take a look at the works of art in the sculpture garden. The one called House of Used Parts, on display spring through fall, includes tires hanging from the ceiling and several ladders. When the weather is nice, you can take your lunch or a snack and eat it in this whimsical little hideaway.

220 E. Chicago Ave.

312/280-2660

 $7 adults, $4.50 students 13 and up; T free

T 10–8, W–Su 10–5

6 and up

Watch for temporary exhibits, which have featured cartoonlike images, large-scale color transparencies of people on Chicago streets, and photographic sculptures. Exhibits are usually accompanied by free gallery guides, guided tours, and films about the artist, which, though not geared to children, can be enlightening. Pressing buttons on an audio wand ($1 rental) reveals information about various artworks. It's a magical way to decipher the language of contemporary art.

Classes for kids include creating puppets, cartoons, collages, or web sites. Free Family Sunday Workshops (fall–spring) are inspired by exhibitions or perhaps holidays. Other items of interest include a summer arts camp, 24-hour Summer Solstice Festival, Family Halloween Benefit, daytime performances for children, chalk-drawing on the plaza, and hands-on creation stations, where kids can make masks and costumes to wear in an extravagant parade led by the life-size puppets and stilt-walkers of Redmoon Theater. Who said art museums were boring?

KID-FRIENDLY EATS The MCA's restaurant is called **Puck's** (tel. 312/397–4034), in honor of Wolfgang Puck, who created the menu. Seasonal items include classics from one of his other restaurants (Spago) and dishes inspired by artworks at the museum. Kids will find pizza, sandwiches, and yummy desserts. You can eat on the terrace overlooking the sculpture garden.

KEEP IN MIND Not all temporary exhibits are appropriate for children, so call in advance to find out. In addition, some works in the permanent collection contain nudity, deal with adult subject matter, or contain language that you might consider a no-no for your kids, and it's not always easy to avoid them. You might want to discuss this possibility with your children beforehand. After all, the goal of some contemporary artists is to be provocative, so use this as an opportunity for conversation.

MUSEUM OF HOLOGRAPHY

18

Laser technology and art intersect at holography, a relatively new technique whose advancement is the focus of this museum, founded in 1976. Housed in a building west of the Loop, in what used to be an out-of-the-way area and is now becoming gentrified, the museum has a collection of holograms, the equipment for making them, and a school of holography. It's perhaps the only museum of its kind in the country, or maybe the world.

Most kids have seen holograms, those 3-D images on credit cards and stickers, many of which seem to shift when you look at them from different angles. These images are created when light waves are reflected from an object illuminated by the light from lasers and recorded on a light-sensitive medium. This complex technique was discovered accidentally in 1948, but it wasn't until the advent of the laser in the '60s that it gained momentum.

The museum has three exhibition spaces, and exhibits change about once a year. Dimly lit for better viewing, galleries usually include works from the permanent collection. One

KEEP IN MIND To help children see holograms best, have them take their time and stand about 5 feet away. The museum isn't usually crowded, so this shouldn't be a problem. To see holograms shift or transform, kids should move slowly from side to side or back and forth.

HEY, KIDS! You'll probably be very tempted to touch the holograms to see if they're "real." But please don't. Fingerprints are a problem on the glass protecting them. And besides, it's against the rules. If you're interested in holography as a career, when you're done with high school, you can attend the museum's school. It takes three 10-week semesters to fully learn how to make holograms, which are used not only by artists, but also in medicine, engineering, architecture, and advertising.

1134 W. Washington Blvd.

 $2.50 ages 6 and up

 W–Su 12:30–5

 6 and up

312/226–1007

awe-inspiring example is a large image of a man bending down to pan for gold. As you walk past it, the gold miner moves his hand, scoops up some water, and looks to see if he has any gold nuggets. The hologram contains about 300 movements in all. Walk back and forth several times to fully appreciate it.

Another impressive hologram is a gigantic *Tyrannosaurus rex* skull with a mouth full of enormous teeth. Because he looks as though he's looming, ready to take a bite, he might frighten some kids. Still other holograms are in transparent cylinders. In one, Michael Jordan seems to turn around and pass a basketball behind his back.

The old saying has it that seeing is believing, and you'll be sorely tempted to believe that many of these holographic images are "real." They're not, of course, and it makes the experience of viewing them downright eerie.

KID-FRIENDLY EATS Once a no-man's-land, this gentrifying neighborhood has attracted trendy restaurants for adults. **Wishbone** (1001 W. Washington Blvd., tel. 312/850–2663) can be recognized by big painted panels of a corncob, pig, and turkey. Its "southern reconstruction" cuisine ranges from corn cakes and blackened catfish to fresh-squeezed orange and carrot juices, and there is outdoor seating.

MUSEUM OF SCIENCE AND INDUSTRY

I mpressive kid-friendly technology starts in the parking garage, home to the *Pioneer Zephyr*. In 1934, this streamlined train, nicknamed the "Silver Streak," made a nonstop run from Denver to Chicago in a record-breaking 13 hours, 4 minutes, and 56 seconds. Your children can hop aboard this first diesel-electric train and feel its rocking motion and then go into the engineer's cab and pretend to be in control. From here it's up the escalator to see a more contemporary form of travel: a replica of the 22-foot-tall Cassini Space Probe, launched in 1997 and scheduled to orbit Saturn in 2004.

But that's just the beginning. At the Coal Mine, an elevator ride simulates a trip deep into the earth, and it's dark down there. At the bottom, a small train like those that miners rode takes you to see what mining was like in the 1930s. Another exhibit takes you "underwater" in a German U-505 submarine from World War II. To discover how the heart works, kids can walk inside a giant model of one. To find out about business, they can head to the Enterprise exhibit, where pedaling the Supply and Demand Cycle reveals where the supply and demand curves meet.

KEEP IN MIND The museum is big, so take breaks to rest, eat, and see an Omnimax movie. (For the same price as the movie, you can opt for an evening Omnilaser Fantasy light show featuring rock music.) To ensure tickets, reserve in advance. Even ticket-holders begin lining up 15–20 minutes early. Many people think the best seats are high up and in the middle. Speaking of tickets, so that the Imagination Station doesn't get too crowded, free, timed tickets are available at the exhibit entrance, and there are rest rooms and a nursing room within the exhibit, so you won't have to leave before you're ready.

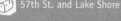

Though most everything in the museum appeals to children, there's also a special area, the Imagination Station, especially for them. If you have an infant, head for an enclosed space with toys where even the smallest scientist can discover the wonders of the world. Children 10 and under can explore light, color, and especially water in an area with a stream that's perfect for floating boats they build or manipulating pumps and wheels, locks and dams. The pièce de résistance is an enormous contraption with levers, cranks, gears, and buttons that produce amazing effects.

No visit to the museum is complete, however, without being enveloped by an Omnimax film depicting the natural wonders of the earth, sky, and sea. It puts science and industry into stunning perspective.

KID-FRIENDLY EATS The museum has a number of places to eat, including a **Pizza Hut;** an **ice-cream parlor,** inside the Yesterday's Main Street exhibit; and the **Astro Cafe.** Near the Omnimax theater, it carries hot dogs, hamburgers, pizza, and nachos. An outdoor patio is open when the weather is willing.

HEY, KIDS! There are a lot of big, spectacular things to see at the museum, but take time for little things, too. One such is the Fairy Castle, which was donated to the museum in 1949 by Hollywood movie star Colleen Moore. Its seven rooms, which have electricity and running water no less, are decorated with tiny treasures.

NAVY PIER

Navy Pier was built in 1916 for commercial ships, but after years of standing unused, it was transformed in 1995 into a place to have fun. Though people do come in winter, summer sees the biggest festivities and the biggest crowds. In fact, it can be a challenge just to stroll the walkways (be sure to keep your children close), but the hustle and bustle can be part of the pleasure.

Vendors sell lemonade, popcorn, cotton candy, and french fries. On weekends your kids can make crafts like masks, hats, and baseball banners free of charge. Wherever you go you'll run into free entertainment by jugglers, magicians, clowns, and groups such as the Navy Pier Players, the Pier Pressure Brass, and an improv group called A Pearing Daily. Navy Pier Follies, a show for families, plays summer Sundays at the open-air Skyline Stage. The carousel has so many unusual hand-painted animals that your kids will find it hard to choose, and the slow-moving Ferris wheel gives everyone time to appreciate the view. Cap off your day with fireworks, given Wednesdays and Saturdays in summer.

HEY, KIDS!

Walk all the way to the end of the pier, and look around you. Do you feel like you're standing in the middle of Lake Michigan? That's not surprising. You've come 3,000 feet out from the shore.

KID-FRIENDLY EATS

Along with other pier eateries (see Chicago Children's Museum), **Bubba Gump Shrimp Co.** (tel. 312/595–5500), inspired by the movie *Forrest Gump*, offers shrimp, burgers, and a box of chocolates. Show the side of the license plate you're given that says "Stop, Forrest, Stop" if you need service, "Run, Forrest, Run" if you're fine. Children work at place mats with Gump-y games or look at movie memorabilia or the film itself, which plays continuously with the sound down. As you leave, take a picture on the bench with Forrest's suitcase and chocolate box.

600 E. Grand Ave.

 Free; various activities extra

 312/595-PIER

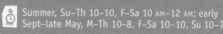 Summer, Su–Th 10–10, F–Sa 10 AM–12 AM; early Sept–late May, M–Th 10–8, F–Sa 10–10, Su 10–7

All ages

The pier is also home to the Chicago Children's Museum (*see above*) and to the Cineplex Odeon's IMAX Theater (tel. 312/595-0090), which shows not only traditional Imax films on its six-story, 80-foot-wide screen, but also 3-D movies.

Inside the pier building, vendors have carts for crafts, such as sand art and candle-making; these are open daily but charge a fee. Take a peek at the free Museum of Stained Glass Windows, where beautiful multicolor windows recovered from buildings that were being torn down paint a picture of Chicago history. Shops galore include the Chicago Children's Museum store, a magic shop, a place that sells crazy hats, and another that does hair wraps and sells glittery nail polish. And in case you think there's nothing new under the sun in winter, come skate on the open-air ice rink.

TRANSPORTATION Parking at Navy Pier is limited and expensive ($6.50 for the first hour). Try to find parking in lots or on the streets west of the museum. It may be several long blocks away, so take the free trolley that runs west on Grand Avenue to Rush Street and then back east on Illinois Street. Another option is to take a CTA bus here: No. 29 State Street, No. 56 Milwaukee Avenue, No. 65 Grand Avenue, No. 66 Chicago Avenue, No. 120 Northwestern Train Station, and No. 121 Union Station.

NEW MAXWELL STREET MARKET

If your children are old enough to appreciate browsing as opposed to buying and won't subject you to an endless stream of "Can I have . . . ," then a Sunday spent at this open-air market can be a great family outing. The first Maxwell Street Market developed in a Jewish neighborhood in the early 1900s. Vendors pushed carts full of merchandise and sold fruits and vegetables from stands in the streets. Though the first location was gobbled up by urban development, a new market grew up nearby in 1994. It is as much a piece of urban folklore as it is a place of commerce, and people come to rummage through new and used stuff alike in search of bargains and hidden antiques.

The market is a microcosm of Chicago, a concept that will probably be lost on children younger than observant teens. Recent and not-so-recent immigrants—plenty of Spanish-speaking people, some Asians, and African-Americans—try to catch hold of the American dream or just earn some ready cash. Senior citizens try to scrounge for a few extra dollars. Your children can uncover brand-new toys and ones that have been slightly abused, new and used video games,

TRANSPORTATION If you buy bulky items, you'll need a car, but as always, driving and parking aren't easy. Canal Street around the market is closed, but side streets are manageable. Parking options include lots on 14th Place between Clinton and Canal streets and at the River West Plaza at Roosevelt Road and Jefferson Street, metered parking on Roosevelt between Clinton and Des Plaines, and free diagonal parking on Clinton between Taylor and Roosevelt. Free diagonal parking is also available April–October on Clinton between Polk and Taylor and on Des Plaines from Taylor to Roosevelt.

stuffed animals, and used bikes. There are small trinkets like key chains with cartoon characters and refrigerator magnets that play jingles. There are clothes and shoes for all ages, as well as such necessities as toilets and car tires. The pleasure is in the search.

Musicians perform and pass the hat, and chances are good that you'll hear some blues—a staple of the market for years—along with Peruvian flute and perhaps some alternative rock. A sketch artist sometimes sets up an easel. But kids just like to soak up the activity and maybe dream of finding that special treasure.

KID-FRIENDLY EATS Not surprisingly, the food sold at stands here is eclectic. There are hot dogs and Polish sausage, steak burgers, tacos, and egg rolls. In warm weather, you can get ice cream.

KEEP IN MIND There is a lot of hustle and bustle here. In fact, approximately 20,000 people come to the market every Sunday, so warn your kids to stay close so as not to get lost. Should you become separated, advise them to seek out one of the market's zone managers, who wear a New Maxwell Street Market badge on their shirts or jackets, or a security officer with a badge. Set up a clear meeting spot and time with older kids who are allowed to go off on their own; it gets far too crowded to count on running into each other.

NORTH BRANCH BICYCLE TRAIL

This 20-mile Cook County Forest Preserve Trail stretches from Chicago all the way north to Lake County through a variety of landscapes. The paved trail, made especially for families, is flat or gently sloping—no Tour de France, here.

The trail traverses Caldwell Woods along the North Branch of the Chicago River. Just north of Devon Avenue at the beginning of the trail, a flatwoods area contains old pin oaks and swamp white oaks as well as spring flowers such as trillium, trout lily, and wild geranium. The area between Devon and Touhy avenues is a savanna, common in Illinois 200 years ago.

The trail continues past the summertime swimmers at Whealan Aquatic Center (one place where trail access is near parking) and on through Miami Woods in Skokie and Linne Woods in Morton Grove. The trail through Miami Woods, north of Oakton Street, passes by the eastern edge of an approximately 20-acre natural prairie—a slice of Illinois as it was before settlers arrived. Grasses grow, and in August the flowering stalks are over 6 feet tall.

KID-FRIENDLY EATS To make your outing complete, take along a picnic lunch. If you'd prefer, though, you can ride to the Chicago Botanic Garden (*see above*), which has a café with outdoor seating.

KEEP IN MIND Call ahead to get a trail map. Then read the rules for biking and explain them to your children. Stay to the right, and ride single file, warning others before you pass. Obey all stop signs. The speed limit is 8 mph, and no racing is allowed. Children should not disturb the native landscape. Flowers should not be picked, and fallen trees should be left where they are, to make good homes and food for wildlife and nourish the soil, too. If you go for a walk, stay on the paths, or you may encounter poison ivy.

From Caldwell and Devon Aves. to Chicago Botanic Garden, Lake Cook Rd., Glencoe

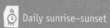 Free

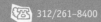 312/261-8400

 Daily sunrise–sunset

All ages

Next comes the Chick Evans Golf Course and Harms Woods, just north of Golf Road, where you might see horseback riders on their own trail, parallel to the bike path. Stables are nearby. Continue on to Glenview and Blue Star Memorial woods before arriving at the Skokie Lagoons, created by the Civilian Conservation Corps during the Depression. The lagoons, where people go canoeing and rowing, are home to sandpipers, egrets, and heron. Farther north, the trail ends at the formal Chicago Botanic Garden (*see above*).

If you've gotten the idea that the trail threads through pure nature, without housing developments and office buildings, you're right. All along it are places to picnic, rest, and drink well water. Pick a section of path or ride it all if you want to, but bike it again at different times of year to see the landscape change.

HEY, KIDS! Though the trail is home to possums, raccoons, beaver, mink, muskrats, and owls you won't see them by day. More likely are rabbits, gray and fox squirrels, and chipmunks. Deer here are fearless. Since much of their natural habitat has been developed, the areas along the bike trail have become their home and their pathway along the river. You might also hear warblers. If you stop and walk to the river, you can see ducks, various turtles, and green and bull frogs.

NORTH PARK VILLAGE NATURE CENTER

This nature preserve is a haven, both for wildlife and the humans who come here to take a break from civilization. Four ecosystems are contained within it—wetland, oak savanna, prairie, and woodland—and the vegetation you and your children will find as you walk from one ecosystem to another varies widely.

Over 7,000 native plants grow in front of the nature center in gardens that represent a microcosm of the preserve's ecosystems, but there are also three other gardens. In one, plants such as wild bergamot and prairie blazing star have been chosen because they attract black swallowtails, monarchs, and other butterflies. A Native American garden, with a realistic tepee nearby, is made up of such plants as pale purple coneflower and goldenseal, which Native Americans used in medicines. A vegetable garden features plants you can grow in your own backyard.

The preserve's natural habitats are also home to toads, turtles, salamanders, rabbits, deer, and lots of birds, so your kids should keep an eye peeled. If you come at the right time, you

HEY, KIDS! Pay your respects to the center's green heron, who lives in a cage outdoors in summer and indoors when the weather gets cold. He was brought here 20 years ago with an injured wing and has stayed because he couldn't survive in the wild. Though his long beak is made for fishing, he doesn't have to do his own anymore. Staff members feed him live fish each morning. You might spy a heron in one of the preserve's ponds.

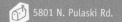 5801 N. Pulaski Rd.

 312/744-5472

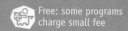 Free; some programs charge small fee

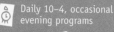 Daily 10–4, occasional evening programs

 All ages

can get help in your explorations from the nature center staff and performers, who regularly offer such family events as spider walks, turtle programs, and campfire storytelling and sing-alongs. Free seasonal events, such as those honoring maple sugaring, Earth Month, the fall harvest, and the winter solstice, include crafts, games, and storytelling.

If your children didn't see enough on the trails or want to get a preview of coming attractions before your walk, venture inside the nature center, where you can get a close-up look at some of the types of small animals that live in the surrounding environment. Indoor and outdoor beehives show how bees live and why they make honey. An outdoor bird aviary contains some examples of the feathered friends that live in the preserve or that stop by on their way north or south. The nature center is a nice place for your family to stop by, too.

KID-FRIENDLY EATS The center has several picnic tables as well as a grassy space in the shade of an oak tree, but there is no food available at the center. For a fast bite to eat nearby, look for a **McDonald's** (3241 W. Peterson Ave., tel. 773/588–8860) and an **Arby's** (2938 W. Peterson Ave., tel. 773/761–9438).

KEEP IN MIND After you've seen the gardens here, think about whether you'd like to add any of these plants to your backyard. Native plants are good choices, because they're so well adapted to this climate. Flowers and other plants that attract birds and butterflies can produce fascinating activity along with color. Besides, it's fun to garden with more than "looks" in mind.

ORIENTAL INSTITUTE MUSEUM

This museum is housed in a three-story neo-Gothic building similar to the other buildings on the University of Chicago campus. Its five galleries devoted to ancient civilizations were closed in 1996 to install climate-control systems to protect the precious artifacts and to create more open exhibit spaces.

The first gallery to reopen (in 1998) was the Egyptian Gallery, where a colossal 17-foot statue of King Tutankhamen towers over everyone (including Michael Jordan if he were to come). Your children can walk around Tut, noticing all the things he wears that are different from what men wear today: a pleated skirt, a dagger with a falcon head, a striped head cloth, and a cobra rearing up on his forehead, supposedly for protection. Other objects in the gallery reveal similarities between the ancient Egyptians and us. There are statues of a police chief, a candy-maker, and several bakers as well as jewelry that most women would be happy to wear today, except perhaps for the extra-large earrings. There is also a tunic and a pair of shoes worn by an Egyptian child long ago, and Egyptian games include one carved like

HEY, KIDS! The museum has some worksheets to help you learn more about the ancient civilizations. Ask for a guide to help you explore the signs and symbols on the coffins and mummies in the Egyptian Gallery. You'll find out that an eye stands for health and a scarab beetle symbolizes regeneration. See if you can find these images on other objects in the exhibition.

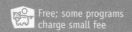
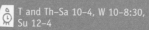

a coiled snake, its body divided into segments. Adult mummies are here, but so is an intricately wrapped one of a child, demonstrating how much children were valued in ancient Egypt. Have your kids look for the mummy of a crocodile. It's partially unwrapped so the head is visible.

Artifacts from the museum's ancient Mesopotamian collection, including a 40-ton (yes, 40-ton) bull and wall sculptures depicting the king, his servants, and soldiers, are expected to be in place by early 2001. Exhibits documenting the ancient civilizations of Persia, Nubia, Turkey, and Israel should be open by 2003.

Family days occur four times a year. One in summer is held in conjunction with the Smart Museum, which houses a collection of Oriental and European art, and at Halloween the Mummies Night is very popular. Hands-on workshops, theatrical performances, and films are also offered.

KID-FRIENDLY EATS The **Reynolds Club** (5706 S. University Ave., tel. 773/702–8787), also in a neo-Gothic campus building, has a food court with pizza, tacos, and Chinese food. A wood-paneled dining room has portraits of university presidents. The **Nile Restaurant** (1611 E. 55th St., tel. 773/324–9499) roams beyond Egypt. Middle Eastern dishes include hummus, stuffed grape leaves, tabbouleh, and shish kebabs. Children like the *shawerma*, marinated, rotisserie-cooked, shredded chicken.

PEACE MUSEUM

"Peacenik" may no longer be a common term, but the effort to give peace a chance is as pertinent now as it was in the '60s. Enter the Peace Museum, which was founded in 1981 by Chicago artist Mark Rogovin and Marjorie Craig Benton, U.S. ambassador to UNICEF at the time. They sought to show how activists and artists have worked and continue to work for peace worldwide and how all people can learn to live their lives peacefully. In a redbrick building that was a factory but now comprises lofts, the museum holds four changing exhibits a year and has 10,000 artworks, artifacts, and historical items in its permanent collection. Some are always on display; others rotate.

Exhibits have included those on Martin Luther King, Jr.; domestic violence; and the nuclear and environmental destruction of the earth. In opposition to drive-by shootings, the museum mounts the annual Drive-by-Peace exhibit in spring and early summer, displaying kids' artwork. Children's activities change from year to year but usually include the Drive-by-Peace board game, which helps them discover the seven steps to conflict resolution. The exhibit

HEY, KIDS! In the permanent collection, you can always see a guitar that belonged to John Lennon, who wanted everyone to give peace a chance, and a statue of a seated man looking over his shoulder for nuclear bombs. You can also ask a staff member to bring out objects not on display. Popular ones include manuscripts of the songs "New Year's Day" and "Sunday, Bloody, Sunday," by U2's Bono, and of the poem "Dreams in a Box," which he wrote especially for the museum. It ends "I am a word writer . . . but it is actions man-made and concrete that we need . . ."

314 W. Institute Pl.

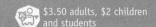 $3.50 adults, $2 children and students

 T-Sa 11–5

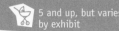 312/440–1860

5 and up, but varies by exhibit

also includes art activities. Older visitors might create books listing their own seven steps to peace. Young children might play a game called Packing My Suitcase for a Peaceful Planet, which asks them to draw a picture of the objects they would choose. Very young children might find a corner with nonviolent toys.

In the library, look at the more than 100 books, listen to a tape, or watch the video about the Japanese girl Sadako, who contracted leukemia after being exposed to radiation from the atom bomb dropped on Hiroshima during World War II. She believed in the legend that good health will come to those who fold 1,000 origami cranes but died before completing her task. Other Japanese children made the remaining birds and collected enough money to build a statue of her holding a golden crane in the Hiroshima Peace Park. It's a symbol of the desire for peace, as is this museum.

KID-FRIENDLY EATS Families like to eat at big and boisterous **Joe's Crab Shack** (745 N. Wells St., tel. 312/664–2722) for seafood. Lively **Scoozi!** (410 W. Huron St., tel. 312/943–5900) has an open kitchen and a wood-burning oven for pizzas. Its antipasti bar is 12 feet long.

PEDWAY

hicago is hiding something, a not-so-secret system of underground walkways that has become almost a city unto itself, containing stores, restaurants, and other places of business. In the early 1950s the city started building tunnels to connect subway stations, and, like a monster, the Pedway just kept growing. It will probably keep expanding beyond its current size, a warren of 23 blocks that children, and adults, like to explore. As many commuters can attest—they use the Pedway to get between trains or subways and their offices without braving the elements—there are many entrances to this maze. A convenient one is at the State Street subway station, between Randolph and Washington streets. To find other entrances, consult the map, available from the information center in the Chicago Cultural Center (*see above*), which just happens to be above the Pedway. If you're ever lost, just look for an exit and go up to street level, where you'll soon get your bearings.

Walking along the stretch west of State Street, you'll find a little of everything: a newsstand that sells snacks and fresh fruits; a barber shop; a Starbucks; a blind person selling

HEY, KIDS! Here's a fun game: First, make sure your parents get a map of the Pedway. (They'll want one anyway, to navigate the corridors without getting too confused.) Then pause in a spot and try to guess what's above ground there. Try to picture all the people over your head and what they might be doing. Your parents can look at the map and tell you if you're right.

 State of Illinois Center to Swissôtel

 Free

 312/744–2400 for maps

M–F rush hour–rush hour; some
sections open Sa

6 and up

newspapers; a big gift store with stuffed animals, balloons with messages on them, and gourmet suckers in unusual flavors; and a food court with an eclectic selection.

If you go east from State Street, you'll pass by the lower level of Marshall Field's and then on down a hallway with lots of shops. Beneath the Chicago Cultural Center, your children can look through the window of a radio station, where people are broadcasting books for the blind to listen to. Farther along, at the Athletic Club, kids can see a seven-story climbing wall; come at lunchtime to see office workers work out.

Like a city, the Pedway seemingly has neighborhoods. The eastern section, which travels under several hotels, is the most elegant and has a shopping concourse. Also like a city, the Pedway is a good place to simply wander, discovering surprises all along the way.

KID-FRIENDLY EATS On the Pedway's west side, on the Daley Center lower level, **West Egg Cafe** (66 W. Washington St., tel. 312/ 236–3322) specializes in omelets for breakfast, but it serves other meals, too. Kids like the gourmet pancakes, including Strawnana Cakes and Berried Treasures. **Houlihan's** (111 E. Wacker Dr., tel. 312/616–FOOD) has a standard kid's menu.

PEGGY NOTEBAERT NATURE MUSEUM

This nature museum, founded in 1857 as the Chicago Academy of Sciences, is the oldest museum in Chicago, but that doesn't mean it's over the hill. In fact, its brand-new building near the Lincoln Park Zoo (*see* listing for parking suggestions) has many new exhibits as well as some old favorites.

One much-loved exhibit is the Butterfly Haven, where no butterfly nets are needed. As your children stroll through, they'll see all sorts of these beautiful creatures: orange-colored pearl crescents, painted ladies, red admirals, and black swallowtails with wings edged in blue and purple—all of whom live in the Midwest. Youngsters can watch the butterflies feed and find chrysalises, caterpillars, and eggs (with a magnifying glass).

Kids learn more about the Midwest at the Water Lab, featuring a model of a river. They can create acid rain; learn about Lake Michigan's inhabitants, including undesirable zebra mussels and alewives; and look at drops of water through a microscope. In City Science, your family

HEY, KIDS! Once you've learned something about nature in the Midwest, go out on one of the museum's terraces and see if you can spot five different ecological communities—prairie, pond, ravine, moist woodland, and dunes—in the surrounding landscape.

Fullerton Pkwy. and Cannon Dr.

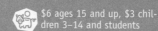
773/549-0606

$6 ages 15 and up, $3 children 3–14 and students

M–T and Th–Su 10–5 (to 6 Memorial Day–Labor Day), W 10–8

3 and up

can find out who else lives in your house with you. You'll learn the difference between good and bad bacteria and see what lurks beneath your basement. The well-liked dioramas are back in an area called the Wilderness Walk, where you travel through Illinois's ecosystems.

Anyone with young children should head to the Children's Gallery. Chances are they'll be overjoyed to put on a beaver costume, enter a beaver lodge, and explore underground tunnels, finding out firsthand about these famed tree gnawers. They can play among the soft-sculpture flowers and tall grasses of a make-believe prairie and search a mural to find well-camouflaged animals. In a setting purported to be under a prairie, they can see the roots of prairie plants overhead and learn about the snakes and ant colonies that dwell underground. And if anyone gets tired, you can rest in comfortable areas nearby and read a book.

KID-FRIENDLY EATS The museum's **Butterfly Cafe** doesn't serve hot dogs and hamburgers, but it does turn out plenty of sandwiches made with fresh ingredients. For other eating options, *see* the Lincoln Park Zoo.

KEEP IN MIND To give your children the best chance of seeing butterflies up close, remind them to be as quiet and still as possible in the Butterfly Haven. These beauties are skittish and don't tend to stick around when loud and boisterous youngsters are being loud and boisterous.

RAINBOW FALLS WATER PARK

Water, water everywhere, and all of it's for play. This water park and adjacent miniature golf course cover 5½ acres. Your kids won't know where to start splashing and sliding first. They can rush pell-mell down three different flume slides or climb up a platform made of make-believe boulders to dive into an L-shape pool. The Lazy River isn't completely lazy; after swirling along for 300 feet, floaters head down chutes to a splash landing. Water cannons await pretend pirates, and tunnels await those seeking to hide from the scoundrels. Young Tarzans and Janes can swing through the air, landing not in a jungle, but in refreshing water.

The welcome mat's always out at the cheery, three-story, purple, yellow, and turquoise Funhouse. It's just like a carnival fun house, with surprises when you least expect them. Just when kids thought it was safe to get back out of the water, someone might spray them—or perhaps they'll dump a bucketfull on someone else. The atmosphere of suspense is heightened by a big bowl on the roof, 32 feet above, which slowly fills with water and then every few minutes, tips over, spilling it on everyone below. For more action, a tube ride hurtles kids down

KEEP IN MIND Contrary to what you might think, weekdays at the water park are the most crowded, because busloads of campers come to play. So weekends are actually the best times for families. Waits are usually no more than several minutes for each activity. The park has showers and changing areas.

KID-FRIENDLY EATS The **Splash Cafe** concession stand has quick snacks, such as popcorn and pretzels, and easy-to-eat meals like pizza and nachos. There are tables shaded by umbrellas as well as some grassy areas with picnic tables nearby. If you want a more peaceful time-out, you can take your food and climb aboard the River Queen, a replica of a Mississippi River paddleboat, to eat. If you prefer, instead of buying food at the concession stand, you can bring your own picnic.

100 Lions Dr., Elk Grove Village

 $8 adults, $7 children 2–17; miniature golf $3

 847/228-2860

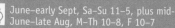 June–early Sept, Sa–Su 11–5, plus mid-June–late Aug, M–Th 10–8, F 10–7

 2 and up

80 feet into a cool pool. Older kids love the Funhouse, but so do some parents, particularly when accompanying adventuresome toddlers who giggle with delight.

Little H$_2$O lovers, up to age 7, have places that are meant just for them in the Children's Adventure Pool. There's a junior water slide, a spraying turtle that doubles as a slide, tunnels, and a gentle tube ride. Toddlers can experiment with the water experience just a little bit, but not too much, in a wading pool.

When your kids get waterlogged, it's time for a game of miniature golf. Perhaps too challenging for kids under 5, the course has some difficult holes, some where the hole itself can't be seen from the tee and one where you have to hit the ball over, what else—water.

HEY, KIDS! Some kids like water a lot and some like it just a little, so only splash (or spray) those who want to be splashed, and be gentle with the others. Don't forget that, for safety's sake, running isn't allowed. You have to know how to swim to go on the water slides and the tube rides. Lifeguards keep watch to make sure the rule is adhered to, but that doesn't mean you can't have fun doing all the other activities.

ROSENBAUM ARTIFACT CENTER

The Spertus Museum, with a permanent collection of approximately 10,000 artworks and artifacts, focuses on the history of Jewish religion and culture spanning the globe and the centuries, from antiquity to contemporary times. Children, Jewish and gentile alike, can learn a lot about Judaism here, seeing beautiful objects whose purposes they may or may not be familiar with. But they can discover even more—and on their own—in the museum's Rosenbaum ARTiFACT Center.

Here kids can dig up artifacts in an archaeological mound, with 12 trenches representing different periods from 1280 to 200 BC. They can use digging tools to search the site's layers and a sieve to sift the sand, revealing old coins, pottery shards, and other relics. Kids can then take their finds to an archaeologist's lab and look in drawers representing the different time periods to find other objects and information. The result is a picture of how people lived long ago in the area that is now Israel.

HEY, KIDS! We don't have CDs of the songs Jewish people played centuries ago, but we do know what their musical instruments looked like. You can try out reproductions of 22 ancient instruments and press buttons to hear other people playing them. You'll find materials to make your own drum out of a coffee tin, a rattle by enclosing dry macaroni in a paper cup, and a lyre with cardboard and rubber bands. Try making up your own tune, too.

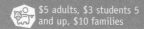

In Family Life at the Oasis, youngsters go back 2,500 years to the time when Israelites, who had been exiled by the Babylonians, returned to their land. Kids open doors in a map to find answers to questions children asked their parents on their journey home. This is the place to discover what Israelites used to heal wounds and what children did when they were bored. If you listen, you'll hear the sounds of birds, the wind, laughter, and a flute.

The Israelite House is designed for preschoolers. Here little ones can look for artifacts in a site meant for little hands, climb onto a make-believe camel, try on clothing, pretend to bake bread in a small oven, and make up stories and perform them with puppets. Special activities, for which there's an additional fee (usually $5), are scheduled regularly and may include making scenes from ancient Israel inside a shoe box, a house sculpture out of clay, or a woven bag. Children become time travelers, and their pretend games re-create bygone eras.

KID-FRIENDLY EATS **Trattoria Caterina** (616 S. Dearborn St., tel. 312/939–7606) has a children's menu with Italian flair that includes pizza, pasta with butter, or pasta marinara with a meatball. For a snack of lemon or turtle cookies and juice, try **Gourmand** (728 S. Dearborn St., tel. 312/427–2610). See Chicago Playworks for other choices.

KEEP IN MIND If your kids are 12 or older, you might want to visit the Zell Holocaust Memorial in the Spertus Museum. It's not designed with children in mind, however, so the artifacts, photos, and video might be too disturbing for sensitive youths. It's best to prepare your kids for the experience beforehand and accompany them throughout.

RYERSON WOODS

6

Ryerson Woods is two things in one. It's both a beautiful natural setting and a farm with domesticated animals. Start by getting a map at the visitor center, a lovely Greek Revival mansion built by the Edward L. Ryerson family, who donated property for part of this conservation area in 1966. (In subsequent years, other families donated land to the Lake County Forest Preserve, which purchased some itself, and 550-acre Ryerson Woods opened in 1972.) With map in hand, start a careful exploration of this environmentally sensitive land.

Junior naturalists will enjoy walking along 6 miles of trails through land that is home to over 150 kinds of birds and 500 different plants. One trail meanders through a forest and along the banks of the Des Plaines River, so animals can be spotted both on land and over the water. Another trail, which is wheelchair accessible, goes through the prairie and along the edge of the woods. The visitor center provides a tape, which can be used free of charge, that points out interesting details along this trail.

HEY, KIDS!
Take a look in the two log cabins, which have exhibits that change according to the seasons. Here you will be able to touch a beaver skin and the antler of a deer and look closely at an owl prepared by a taxidermist. Pretty neat, huh?

KEEP IN MIND Ryerson Woods is the habitat for many endangered species, including the purple-fringed orchid, dog violets, the red-shouldered hawk, and the Eastern Massasauga rattlesnake. (Never fear, these snakes live far from the trails and avoid contact with humans.) As a result, the familiar motto—Take nothing but pictures, leave nothing but footprints—applies here. Picking and collecting plants is prohibited, as are pets, picnics, fishing, horses, bicycles, and snowmobiles. It's important to stay on the trails to protect the very rare woodland as well as to avoid poison ivy.

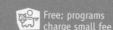 21950 N. Riverwoods Rd., Deerfield

 847/948–7750

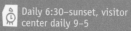 Free; programs charge small fee

 Daily 6:30–sunset, visitor center daily 9–5

All ages

For a different experience, head to Ryerson's barn, where your children can hear the real versions of Old McDonald's farm sounds. The turkey goes "gobble, gobble"; the sheep says "baa, baa"; and some chickens, pigs, cows, and a goat add their own distinctive voices to the chorus.

Depending on the time of year you visit, there will be something different to see and do. The maple forest is splendid in the fall. In early summer, a small piece of prairie is a field of tall grasses, but by late summer its flowers are in full bloom. Cross-country skiers are welcome in the winter whenever there is at least 4 inches of snow. Annual events, ranging from sheep shearing to a Halloween Hike, and less elaborate family programs are held throughout the year. But whenever you visit, Ryerson Woods is a great place to get to know Mother Nature firsthand.

KID-FRIENDLY EATS Picnics aren't allowed at Ryerson Woods. For '50s nostalgia and food, try **Ed Debevic's Short Order Deluxe** (*see above*). **Flatlander's** (Milwaukee Ave. and Old Half Day Rd., Lincolnshire, tel. 847/821–1234), in a setting inspired by Frank Lloyd Wright's Prairie style, has lots of kid fare, finished with a root-beer float or a sundae in a waffle-cone bowl. The **Northbrook Court Shopping Center food court** (2171 Lake Cook Rd., Northbrook, tel. 847/498–1770) has the usual.

SEARS TOWER SKYDECK

5

Like the Hancock Center, which predated it by three years, the 1,450-foot Sears Tower (1973) was the tallest building in the world for a while, until the spire-topped Petronas Towers were built in Kuala Lumpur, Malaysia, in 1996. Chicago fans can still take pride in the Sears Tower's 110 stories (to the Petronas Towers' paltry 88) and in yet another spectacular view.

Pause in the waiting area to look at the model of Chicago, a preview of what you'll see from on high, and a video about the history of the city and the Sears Tower. Next, board the elevator to the Skydeck, but hold onto your ears and your stomach, as the elevator travels at 1,600 feet per minute. On a clear day, four states are visible from the observation deck: Indiana, Michigan, Wisconsin, and, of course, Illinois, as well as the beautiful blue expanse of Lake Michigan. But your children might begin to wonder whether the elevator magically transported you all into a new Rick Moranis movie—*Honey, I Shrunk Chicago*—as everything is so far below that it looks miniature. Help them try to locate familiar landmarks, such as the United Center (where the Bulls play), various museums, and Chicago's third-tallest building, the John

KID-FRIENDLY EATS In the Sears Tower, only **Sbarro** (tel. 312/382–8500) is open weekends. Weekdays try **Dos Hermanos** (tel. 312/993–0527), for Mexican food; **Eadie's Kitchen** (tel. 312/993–0493), for turkey burgers and veggie pockets; the Italian **Mia Torre** (tel. 312/474–1350); or **Mrs. Levy's Deli** (tel. 312/993–0530) and her irresistible ice cream. (These are reached via a different lobby.) A food court featuring healthy items should open in the Skydeck area in spring 2000. Another weekend option is the large, bustling **Greek Islands** (200 S. Halsted St., tel. 312/782–9855).

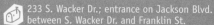

233 S. Wacker Dr.; entrance on Jackson Blvd. between S. Wacker Dr. and Franklin St.

Mar–Sept, daily 9–11; Oct–Feb, daily 9–10

 312/975–9696

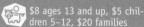 $8 ages 13 and up, $5 children 5–12, $20 families

 All ages

Hancock Center. Looking through a telescope is likely to reveal even more recognizable places—maybe even your own neighborhood.

Several holidays are celebrated annually, some with an added bonus. For Red, White and View, the Skydeck's Independence Day celebration, visitors wearing red, white, and blue or clothing with an American flag on it pay half-price admission, as do those who come in costume for the Spook-tacular (guess when?).

The Skydeck is undergoing a multimillion-dollar renovation, scheduled to be finished in spring 2000. New additions include interactive exhibits, both in the waiting area and on the Skydeck level, showing visitors all the hows and wows of the building and its construction, the history of Chicago, and contemporary facts. The aim is to add an eye-opening learning experience to the eye-popping view.

HEY, KIDS! Here's some tantalizing tower trivia: The last beam was signed by 12,000 construction workers, Sears employees, and other Chicagoans. The building's steel frame weighs 76,000 tons, making it practically wind-proof, so don't worry if it sways a bit. And don't worry about window washers, either. Eight times a year, the more than 16,000 windows are cleaned by robots.

KEEP IN MIND At least 5,000 people visit Skydeck daily, so expect a wait: 30–45 minutes on a busy day, though renovations might reduce it. The midday hours (11–3) are the busiest, as are Monday and Friday, so to avoid crowds, go Tuesday–Thursday. For two views for the price of one, arrive just before dusk so you can see the city in daylight; watch the sunset, which can be spectacular; and stay for Chicago after dark, when twinkling lights transform it into a wonderland. It's not a problem; you can stay "on top" of Chicago as long as you want.

SIX FLAGS GREAT AMERICA

Daredevils and fraidy cats can both have fun here. Risk-takers find the screams and heart palpitations they're seeking on the Raging Bull roller coaster, which travels up a 20-story hill before plunging down a 65° drop into a tunnel at more than 70 mph. If this hasn't taken their breath away, maybe the twists and turns will. No wonder it's called a mega- or hyper-coaster. Other giants include ShockWave, with seven loops; the Viper, reaching 100 feet; and the American Eagle, at 127 feet. The 1992 Batman coaster seems like child's play by comparison, but it's worth a ride for nostalgia's sake or for coaster-kids-in-training. For another adrenaline rush, try Splashwater Falls, where (surprise, surprise) boats plunge into water. Everyone gets wet, but that's the point. In warm weather, you dry off fast.

Younger kids head to kinder, gentler rides. The double-decker carousel is awesome, but your children might have trouble deciding which of the 88 horses and 15 other mounts to ride. They'll feel right at home in Looney Tunes National Park, where they'll be greeted by old friends Bugs Bunny, Daffy Duck, and Taz and find a net climb and a train ride around

HEY, KIDS! If you've been to Great America before and think you have done everything there is to do, ask your parents if you can go during October Fright Fest—that is, if you think you won't be scared. The park is decorated for Halloween, and you're sure to encounter all sorts of creepy people.

KEEP IN MIND If you're going with multiple children, take multiple adults in case one child wants you to go on a ride but another won't go along. Explain height restrictions beforehand, so kids are prepared for disappointment. Point out security officers, hosts, and hostesses, so your kids know whom to look for if they (or you) get lost, and familiarize yourself with the location of the Lost Parents station in the Hometown Park. Don't forget sunscreen, but travel light or store your belongings in lockers. And take snack breaks or entertainment breaks so no one gets to the breaking point.

Off I–94 at Grand Ave. east exit, Gurnee

 847/249–INFO

$39 over 48″, $19.50
children age 3–48″

 Late Apr–Oct, Sa–Su 10–5, 6, 7, 8, 9, or
10, plus M–F 10–10 mid–June–mid–Aug

3 and up

cartoon land. Scooby Doo and the Flintstones hang out in Camp Cartoon Network. Little kids can feel grown-up when they ride Spacely's Sprocket Rockets, their own roller coaster. Another favorite, Sky Trek Tower takes youngsters calmly up 285 feet to look down on the whole "tiny" park.

There are also opportunities to sit still and be entertained, great when you're tired of nonstop action. Animals rescued from shelters put on a show that's fun for little ones, while Butch Cassidy and the Sundance Kid show off stunts. You can also just stop and listen to a mariachi band or some country music. For a more high-powered experience, take in an IMAX film, sometimes in 3-D; the theater's seats are synchronized to move with the action on screen. In fact, throughout the park you'll see a lot of action while sitting down.

KID-FRIENDLY EATS There is no lack of choices. You can sit down and have fried chicken or buffet-style turkey and roast beef or stick with the simple stuff like pizza, hot dogs, and tacos. Options include **Angelo's Pasta and Pizza,** in Yankee Harbor; **Crazy Buffalo Saloon,** a sit-down restaurant in Southwest Territory; and **Aunt Martha's,** which serves chicken in Hometown Square.

SKATE ON STATE

3

Chicago may be called the Second City, but its outdoor ice-skating rink won't take second place to any others. The Olympic-size rink is nine times bigger than the one at Rockefeller Center in New York City. Its location on State Street, known as Chicago's Great Street and home to two venerable department stores (Marshall Field's and Carson Pirie Scott), makes it a great place to take a break on shopping excursions. And the old-style street lamps and Christmas decorations make it a special place to skate around the holidays.

People can come and skate, but they can also learn a thing or two. There are free drop-in group skating lessons at 9 on Saturday morning. Sometimes as many as 20 would-be skaters show up, sometimes only a few. The lessons are geared to those who come. Olympic medalist Debi Thomas has hosted skating clinics, and gold medalists Katerina Witt and Kristi Yamaguchi have come to perform. In a series of free programs called Ice-Breakers, talented local skaters perform at noon on weekdays. There are occasional speed-skating competitions (this is the Midwest, after all), and hockey players sometimes appear, too.

HEY, KIDS! Don't worry, it's normal to fall down sometimes. Just get up and keep skating. Don't forget that the rules say that you can't link arms to skate together or join hands to skate in a chain. You're not supposed to sit on the rink boards either. Shoes are not allowed on the ice, so your parents are going to have to wear skates if they want to help you learn how to skate.

State St. between Washington and Randolph Sts.

 312/744–0812

Free; skate rentals $3 adults, $2 children (double runners available)

 Late Nov–early Mar, daily 9–7:15

2 and up

Those who would rather watch than skate will be relieved to know that the two warming sheds, which are closed on three sides and open on the side overlooking the ice, have heating lamps to keep onlookers toasty warm.

School holidays, weekend days, and lunchtimes during the week are the busiest times. Evenings aren't as crowded, and the atmosphere is festive thanks to lights on the rink and on State Street. "Atmosphere" is also enhanced by landscaping (trees in planters) and the slight Alpine chalet disguise worn by the big trailer where skates are rented. The rink's radio sponsors play music that ranges from classical to pop, with some taped Christmas songs added for good cheer. Don't forget to dress warmly because the rink is not protected from cold, blustery winds. Chicago is the Windy City, too.

KID-FRIENDLY EATS The skating rink has three **concession stands,** which sell coffee, hot chocolate, hot dogs, doughnuts, pretzels, and candy. You can eat in the warming sheds, which have picnic tables.

KEEP IN MIND Since its 1991 opening, the rink's situation has been precarious. The city leases the land from a development company; if it ever chooses to build here, the rink will disappear. A replacement is slated for fall 2001 at Millennium Park, a 24½-acre area between Michigan Avenue, Columbus Drive, and Monroe and Randolph streets. The new sunken rink (Michigan Ave. between Washington and Madison Sts.) will include a warming center, restaurant, skate rental, and rest rooms and can be converted to a stage during warm months.

SKOKIE NORTHSHORE
SCULPTURE PARK

Art in the park reaches monumental proportions at this outdoor display, where 45 contemporary sculptures are spread out over 2 miles. Amazingly, they don't stand out awkwardly from their environment but rather blend into this prairie landscape shaded by beautiful old trees. Even more amazing, there's not a DO NOT TOUCH sign to be seen, and youngsters can discover the joys of exploring art hands-on—literally.

The subject matter of some of the sculptures will be obvious, even to very young children. *Charger I* and *Charger II* are two brightly painted steel horses. *USA Monument* depicts the letters U, S, and A piled up and topped with a knife and fork. *Apple Rocket* is just that, an apple with a rocket where the stem should be. Others may leave you perplexed. A sculpture called *Strike* looks like it could be an anteater's nose. Still others are even more abstract, providing endless opportunities for your children to use their imaginations, guessing at the artworks' meaning and seeing all sorts of objects within them. Only 25% of the sculptures are permanent, however; the rest are on loan and may eventually be replaced.

HEY, KIDS! If you're like most kids, your favorite sculpture will be the bright-colored *New Hope Risin'*. Be sure to check it out. It's near the parking lot, halfway between the Dempster Street and Main Street sections of the park. Made of various recycled objects, it contains numerous whirligigs spinning in the wind. Look closely at its many elements. You might even be inspired to go home, find some recyclables, and make your own sculpture. But do your parents a favor: Make yours smaller.

 East side of McCormick Blvd. between Dempster St. and Touhy Ave., Skokie

 Free

 Daily sunrise–sunset

847/583-8549

 All ages

As for how best to enjoy the park, you have a few choices. Some families take a stroll, stopping at sculptures along the way. Others—mostly local Skokie and Evanston families who tend to pedal leisurely—take to the bike path that runs through the sculpture park, bordered on one side by whizzing cars and on the other by an idyllic tree-lined canal, where fish can occasionally be seen jumping out of the water. But there's no hubbub here. Even though a major thoroughfare runs along one side of this outdoor museum, the park is wide enough so that it's easy to ignore the traffic. The setting is tranquil and free of crowds, but it's not a whispering, tiptoeing, art museum kind of quiet. Grassy areas invite children to romp, while shady spaces call parents to sit and rest. As in children's lives, art and play flow together.

KID-FRIENDLY EATS **Herm's Palace** (3406 Dempster St., tel. 847/673–9757) is a local favorite for hot dogs, charburgers, gyros, nachos, and cheese fries. It has a number of video games, some of which are on the violent side. Part of a family-run chain, **Leona's** (3517 Dempster St., tel. 847/982–0101) has a casual atmosphere for eating pizza, traditional Italian food, or even chicken fingers.

KEEP IN MIND There is a lot for children to see and absorb here, and your kids will probably want to do a fair amount of just plain roaming, too. You might want to break up your visit into two parts, with lunch sandwiched in between. Or even split your exploration into two separate visits. Making this easy is on-site parking at both north and south sections: in the center of the Dempster Street to Main Street area and in the Howard Street to Touhy Avenue stretch.

THOMAS HUGHES CHILDREN'S LIBRARY

After the Great Chicago Fire destroyed most of the city in 1871, Thomas Hughes, a member of the British Parliament and the author of *Tom Brown's School Days,* solicited donations of books for the city. Many well-known authors, including Lewis Carroll, sent copies of their works, and the 8,000 volumes that were collected seeded what would become Chicago's main library, which in 1991 moved here. What's ironic is that, unbeknownst to Mr. Hughes, Chicago didn't even have a library before the fire. Nevertheless, it seems only fitting that the city's children's library should take its name from this optimistic, benevolent man.

The children's library is home to over 100,000 volumes in a very family-friendly setting. There are plenty of child-size tables and chairs and a special reading area for toddlers and their parents. Your children won't have any trouble finding some of the best books in the collection, because Caldecott and Newbery award winners are shelved separately. Kids can request a list of recommended books organized by age, from preschool to eighth grade.

HEY, KIDS! Look for more than 70 objects from children's literature in the Storybook Dollhouse. Some are from well-known books, poems, and nursery rhymes; others are more obscure. The peach from *James and the Giant Peach* isn't hard to find, nor is the top hat of the Mad Hatter that Alice encountered. Can you guess what book the silver shoes come from? You may be surprised. In the movie *The Wizard of Oz,* Dorothy wears ruby slippers, but in the book they're silver.

Harold Washington Library Center,
400 S. State St.

 Free

 312/747–4200

M, W, and F–Sa 9–5, T and Th 11–7,
Su 1–5

 3–13

A special fund established NatureConnections, a collection of books, magazines, and videos about natural history, including dinosaurs, of course. A Learning Center has computers, and a Program Room is the site of free special activities on Saturday, including author readings and book signings, jugglers, magicians, and concerts. Toddler story times, which include storytelling, puppetry, music, and theater, are offered on a weekday once a week for six weeks. One-hour Storytime Extravaganzas, for ages 3–5 and 6–8, are scheduled each month. In addition, the fund that established the NatureConnections book collection also funds a series of monthly programs about natural history, usually on Saturday afternoon. Workshops range from making terrariums and bird feeders to presentations by Lincoln Park Zoo staff, who bring in small mammals and reptiles. The library also has a summer reading program with a different theme each year. You don't have to travel very far to find a world full of adventure at the library.

KEEP IN MIND

Children can get a library card of their own as soon as they can print their full name. If your child is just learning to write, why not practice before making a trip to the library? A parent or legal guardian must cosign and show a piece of identification with name and Chicago address.

KID-FRIENDLY EATS

The library's **Beyond Words Cafe** (tel. 312/747–4680) serves both a cold and hot buffet, Monday–Saturday 11–3. In addition, children can choose soup and half a sandwich or a bagel with cream cheese. The **Berghoff** (17 W. Adams St., tel. 312/427–3170) is more than 100 years old, so it's worth seeing for history's sake. Its menu offers a lot of German classics and some American ones, too. For more options, *see* Chicago Playworks.

games

THE CLASSICS

"I'M THINKING OF AN ANIMAL..." With older kids you can play 20 Questions: Have your leader think of an animal, vegetable, or mineral (or, alternatively, a person, place, or thing) and let everybody else try to guess what it is. The correct guesser takes over as leader. If no one figures out the secret within 20 questions, the first person goes again. With younger children, limit the guessing to animals and don't put a ceiling on how many questions can be asked. With rivalrous siblings, just take turns being leader. Make the game's theme things you expect to see at your day's destination.

"I SEE SOMETHING YOU DON'T SEE AND IT IS BLUE." Stuck for a way to get your youngsters to settle down in a museum? Sit them down on a bench in the middle of a room and play this vintage favorite. The leader gives just one clue—the color—and everybody guesses away.

FUN WITH THE ALPHABET

"I'M GOING TO THE GROCERY..." The first player begins, "I'm going to the grocery and I'm going to buy... " and finishes the sentence with the name of an object, found in grocery stores, that begins with the letter "A". The second player repeats what the first player has said, and adds the name of another item that starts with "B". The third player repeats everything that has been said so far and adds something that begins with "C" and so on through the alphabet. Anyone who skips or misremembers an item is out (or decide up front that you'll give hints to all who need 'em). You can modify the theme depending on where you're going that day, as "I'm going to X and I'm going to see..."

"I'M GOING TO ASIA ON AN ANT TO ACT UP." Working their way through the alphabet, players concoct silly sentences stating where they're going, how they're traveling, and what they'll do.

FAMILY ARK   Noah had his ark—here's your chance to build your own. It's easy: Just start naming animals and work your way through the alphabet, from antelope to zebra.

WHAT I SEE, FROM A TO Z   In this game, kids look for objects in alphabetical order—first something whose name begins with "A", next an item whose name begins with "B", and so on. If you're in the car, have children do their spotting through their own window. Whoever gets to Z first wins. Or have each child play to beat his own time. Try this one as you make your way through zoos and museums, too.

JUMP-START A CONVERSATION

WHAT IF...? Riding in the car and waiting in a restaurant are great times to get to know your youngsters better. Begin with imaginative questions to prime the pump.

• If you were the tallest man on earth, what would your life be like? The shortest?
• If you had a magic carpet, where would you go? Why? What would you do there?
• If your parents gave you three wishes, what would they be?
• If you were elected president, what changes would you make?
• What animal would you like to be and what would your life be like?
• What's a friend? Who are your best friends? What do you like to do together?
• Describe a day in your life 10 years from now.

DRUTHERS How do your kids really feel about things? Just ask. "Would you rather eat worms or hamburgers? Hamburgers or candy?" Choose serious and silly topics—and have fun!

FAKER, FAKER Reveal three facts about yourself. The catch: One of the facts is a fake. Have your kids ferret out the fiction. Take turns being the faker. Fakers who stump everyone win.

KEEP A STRAIGHT FACE

"HA!" Work your way around the car. First person says "Ha." Second person says "Ha, ha." Third person says "Ha" three times. And so on. Just try to keep a straight face. Or substitute "Here, kitty, kitty, kitty!"

WIGGLE & GIGGLE Give your kids a chance to stick out their tongues at you. Start by making a face, then have the next person imitate you and add a gesture of his own—snapping fingers, winking, clapping, sneezing, or the like. The next person mimics the first two and adds a third gesture, and so on.

JUNIOR OPERA During a designated period of time, have your kids sing everything they want to say.

IGPAY ATINLAY Proclaim the next 30 minutes Pig Latin time, and everybody has to talk in this fun code. To speak it, move the first consonant of every word to the end of the word and add "ay." "Pig" becomes "igpay," and "Latin" becomes "atinlay." To words that being with a vowel, just add "ay" as a suffix.

MORE GOOD TIMES

BUILD A STORY "Once upon a time there lived..." Finish the sentence and ask the rest of your family, one at a time, to add another sentence or two. Bring a tape recorder along to record the narrative—and you can enjoy your creation again and again.

NOT THE GOOFY GAME Have one child name a category. (Some ideas: first names, last names, animals, countries, friends, feelings, foods, hot or cold things, clothing.) Then take turns naming things that fall into that category. You're out if you name something that doesn't belong in the category—or if you can't think of another item to name. When only one person remains, start again. Choose categories depending on where you're going or where you've been—historic topics if you've seen a historic sight, animal topics before or after the zoo, upside-down things if you've been to the circus, and so on. Make the game harder by choosing category items in A-B-C order.

COLOR OF THE DAY Choose a color at the beginning of your outing and have your kids be on the lookout for things that are that color, calling out what they've seen when they spot it. If you want to keep score, keep a running list or use a pen to mark points on your kids' hands for every item they spot.

CLICK If Cam Jansen, the heroine of a popular series of early-reader books, says "Click" as she looks at something, she can remember every detail of what she sees, like a camera (that's how she got her nickname). Say "Click!" Then give each one of your kids a full minute to study a page of a magazine. After everyone has had a turn, go around the car naming items from the page. Players who can't name an item or who make a mistake are out.

THE QUIET GAME Need a good giggle—or a moment of calm to figure out your route? The driver sets a time limit and everybody must be silent. The last person to make a sound wins.

THEMATIC INDEX

ACKNOWLEDGMENTS

My appreciation goes to Randy Curwen, who had the excellent idea of asking me to write about events for families when hands-on activities first began popping up here and there years ago. I would like to thank my husband, Alain, who is such a good sport and great navigator in my constant search for new activities; and my sons, Stéphane and Théodore, who are always an inspiration, for letting me be the child in the family. I am grateful to all the people in the Chicagoland area who contributed information to this book, for their belief that children are our most precious resource. Many thanks also to editor Andrea Lehman, the queen of the well-placed question mark.

—Nancy Maes

the end